GIVE ME THAT OLD TIME RELIGION!

Who are the faith healers? Itinerant Pentecostal preachers whose ministry includes performing miracles and healing the sick. They attract wide followings with their claims of healing powers and have caused great confusion not only among their followers but also among members of mainline Christian churches.

For an objective overview of these controversial figures, read THE FAITH HEALER. Unlike other books on this subject, THE FAITH HEALER does not attempt to support or refute faith healing, but presents a factual report of the people involved in this movement.

About the Author

Eve Simson is currently an Assistant Professor of Sociology at Indiana University, South Bend, Indiana. She received her M.A. and Ph.D. degrees from Ohio State University. To gather data for this book, she has attended numerous revival meetings and faith healing gatherings. She has personally interviewed the healing evangelists and their followers, the critics and supporters of the faith healing movement.

THE FAITH HEALER

Deliverance Evangelism in North America

Eve Simson

PYRAMID BOOKS ▲ NEW YORK

Pyramid edition published June, 1977

ISBN: 0-515-04405-7

Library of Congress Catalog Card Number: 77–75993

Printed in the United States of America

Pyramid Books are published by Pyramid Publications (Harcourt Brace Jovanovich, Inc.). Its trademarks, consisting of the word "Pyramid" and the portrayal of a pyramid, are registered in the United States Patent Office.

Pyramid Publications
(Harcourt Brace Jovanovich, Inc.)
757 Third Avenue, New York, N.Y. 10017

To my husband, Thomas, in appreciation for his invaluable contributions

Contents

Chapter 1

Search for a Miracle

The large, black letters on the marquee of a once-popular neighborhood movie theater, now converted to a revival center, announced:

BROTHER FOX REVIVAL
PRAYER FOR THE SICK
NIGHTLY 7:00 PM

Inside a handful of worshipers were scattered throughout the two front rows of dingy seats. They were engrossed by the evangelist who was preaching about the evils of sin and the good life awaiting all those who are reborn. Sporadic shouts of "Amen" and "Hallelujah" echoed through the hollow auditorium.

Seated among this small gathering was Mrs. Cochran, a heavyset woman in her early sixties. She had come to this revival for a special purpose. She wanted healing. Anxiously awaiting the promised prayer for the sick, she was hoping that somehow in this place of worship the remedy for her ailments could be obtained.

All her life Mrs. Cochran had been in good health and actively going about her daily chores until that fateful car accident nearly a year ago, in which she was gravely injured. From that time on she had been suffering from excruciating back pains which, it seemed, nobody could alleviate.

Initially she had been under the care of a physician. However, since her condition failed to improve, she ceased to visit him. It all seemed useless to her, and, besides, she felt awkward and ill at ease in his presence. All she knew was that her suffering continued and that medical science had failed to cure the pain.

"It got so bad I no longer could get up. I'd lay in bed in misery. . . . It was real painful to walk. I would get up only to wash and eat. Sometimes I skipped a meal because it was not worth it as I was tired and the pain got so bad sometimes. I don't know what I'd done without my family's help."

Prior to the accident she had often attended the old-time revivals and vividly remembered the prayer lines. But now there appeared to be no way for her to attend a healing revival. They all were held at a distant part of the city. She herself was too ill to leave the house unaided; her daughter did not know how to drive, and her son-in-law refused to take her to a revival meeting, insisting instead that she go to an experienced physician.

"But doctors scare me. I'm afraid they'll tell me the worst. Everytime I've seen one they told me something bad. I always felt so depressed around them. I believe if God can't heal you, nobody can."

One day, while reading one of the many revival magazines which she was regularly receiving, she noticed an advertisement for a prayer cloth which had been blessed by the evangelist and would be sent free of charge to anyone asking for it. She decided to send in the request and shortly received a reply.

"I ended up getting two blessed cloths. The one I ordered, and then a few days later came a second one from another evangelist, who had prayed over it and sent it out. I put them on my back and knees, and soon I was well enough to take the bus here and have Brother Fox pray for me."

Finally the moment arrived when Brother Fox was to pray for her. He placed his hand on her forehead and implored Jesus to come to her aid and release her from the pain that possessed her body. As she slowly walked back to her seat, she seemed to have been deeply moved by the experience.

"I feel much better," she stated after the service, as she waited in front of the gospel center for the bus to take her back home.

Mrs. Cochran is one of countless Americans that have been turning to faith healers for treatment of their bodily ills. Some of them are basically dilettantes who shop around from one healer to another. They hold ambivalent feelings about the type of treatment they want for their ailments as they drift back and forth between the faith healers and the physicians. But there are also those who unquestioningly place their health and wealth in the hands of the faith healers and exlude even from consideration the possibility of using scientific medicine. Every now and then a case of this nature hits the newsprint, serving as a reminder of the devotedness in which such healing practices may be held.

The Parker Case

On a hot August Sunday in 1973 in Barstow, Calif., an itinerant Mexican-American preacher anointed with oil an 11-year-old boy named Wesley Parker, then laid hands on the youngster and pronounced him cured of his diabetes.

Wesley was joyous and rushed to tell his buddies of his cure. Nevertheless, the next morning he decided to test his blood's sugar content. Finding that it was still positive, he prepared to take his usual medication. Noticing what his son was about to do, the father, an unemployed aerospace electrical technician, quickly grabbed the instruments, squirted out the insulin and broke off the hypodermic needle. Before long the symptoms of Wesley's illness started to reappear. As his condition began to deteriorate, the Parkers' pastor and many of their friends gathered in their home to pray for the recovery of the sick youngster. But the symptoms failed to abate. By the second day Wesley was lapsing into periods of unconsciousness. Thinking that perhaps he should be taking his insulin after all, the mother decided to buy a fresh supply but was dissuaded from doing it by the boy's father. Mr. Parker, who had for some time been a believer in devil possession, stated that at this point he personally had exorcised the demons which he believed had been dwelling in Wesley's body. Now surely he would regain his health.

"I knew when the diabetes is caused by two demons and that we could no longer give insulin without inviting the demons back," the father explained.[1]

The parents continued their prayers.

"We bombarded heaven," said Mrs. Parker. "We prayed without ceasing from Tuesday morning to Wednesday afternoon."[2]

Not all of their friends were in agreement with the Parkers, and their pastor recommended that they call a doctor. Someone finally notified the police. But by then it was too late. When the police arrived at the Parkers' home on Wednesday, Wesley was already dead. He had suffered a painful, lingering death. The parents, however, were unperturbed.

"Wesley is going to be resurrected," the father proclaimed.[3]

He predicted that during the resurrection service Wesley would come back to life. The parents would not permit an autopsy and at first refused to have the body embalmed, though they later consented to it. The mother stated: "Christ is going to have to replace the blood that's full of sugar anyway, so it might as well be embalming fluid. If we hadn't done it, people might say he was in a deep coma and not believe the miracle."[4]

Numerous curiosity seekers as well as supporters of the Parker's showed up for the ceremony at the funeral home chapel. At one point during the service Wesley's three remaining siblings and other children who were present were called to lay hands on the body and shout for him to rise from the coffin. But Wesley remained lifeless. Continuing to hold on to his hope, the father maintained that his son, like Lazarus, would rise from his grave on the fourth day. On the fourth day nothing happened. The Parkers extended their vigil. They still had faith that Wesley would return to them healthy and happy.

Their pastor was horrified at what the Parkers had permitted to transpire. Many of their fellow church members believed that they had erred. Reporters began to swarm around the community. In the midst of all this uproar the local authorities charged the Parkers with manslaughter and child abuse, and their bail was set at $10,000 each. In July 1974 a jury found the Parkers guilty of involuntary manslaughter, and in September they were sentenced to five years on probation. One of the conditions of their probation was that they report to their probation officer any illness or injury affecting their three other children.

The Parker case received nationwide coverage by the news media because of its sensational nature. There are countless less spectacular, unpublicized cases that likewise demonstrate the great dedication with which individuals can hold to their belief in miraculous healing and the enormous strength of their faith in face of the setbacks and adversities they have had to encounter. Yet at the same time their faith and hopes have not had for the great majority of them such negative consequences as occurred in the above case. Many of them have instead come forth to testify to all the wonders they have received through the ministrations of the healers.

13

The Deliverance Evangelists

A commitment to a belief in faith healing has existed in all types of societies from the earliest times in human history to the present day. A great variety of faith-healing systems can be encountered that try to deal with man's search for a miracle. They include the psychic surgeons of the Philippines, Spiritualists, Christian Science practitioners, the Shrine of Lourdes, Norbu Chen, Olga Worrall, and Roxanne Brant to name just a few that are attracting large numbers of devotees. Of all the healers the ones most familiar to the people in this country are the deliverance evangelists. They are the most flamboyant and controversial of the healers, attracting not only dedicated followers but also hostile antagonists. They have become subjects of novels, television shows, documentaries, and exposé literature.

Though deliverance evangelists have become a familiar part of the American religious scene, misconceptions about them continue. Some have grouped them with other evangelists, such as Billy Graham. While significant parallels exist, differences between them warrant a distinction. Some have mistakenly equated them with all fundamentalist groups. Preaching of deliverance evangelists has a strong fundamentalist flavor, but differences between them and many fundamentalist preachers are great enough for the two to be treated as separate entities. Many fundamentalist denominations have been among the severest critics of the deliverance evangelists. In both of the above cases the major trait which sets the deliverance evangelists apart is their involvement in spectacular, emotion-laden public healings of physical ailments.

The deliverance evangelists may be described as one type of itinerant Pentecostal preachers. They preach the Gospel in accordance with "that old-time religion" and

14

disseminate belief in gifts of the Holy Ghost, including the miracle of faith cures as they lay claim to having been given the gift of divine healing. Some of them have received frequent nationwide coverage by the news media, and the name Oral Roberts has become synonymous with faith healing in the minds of many Americans.

Chapter 2

The Hallelujah Trail:
The Emergence of Deliverance Evangelism

"Hallelujah," "Glory to God," "Praise the Lord," shouted the small crowd that had gathered to hear the Word of God in an innocuous tent pitched in Tulsa, Okla. But one man who viewed the scene from across the street sought neither revelation nor salvation. His heart was filled with malice as he contemplated the tall, black-haired young man who was preaching about Jesus and divine healing. The evangelist, fired-up with enthusiasm, did not notice this man, nor did any of the worshipers. The man felt the loaded revolver he was carrying and made up his mind that now was the time to use it. He grasped the gun, aimed at the evangelist, and pulled the trigger. The bullets whizzed toward the unsuspecting evangelist and tore into the canvas about two feet above his head. Luckily the evangelist remained unharmed. The next day newspapers carried an account of the incident. Attention came to be focused on the Pentecostal preacher, Oral Roberts, who stood at the beginning of an amazing career. Later he came to be known as King of the Faith Healers.

A Turning Point for Oral Roberts

One morning more than 20 years after this event I received from Oral Roberts a letter that formally announced another major turn in his life and fortunes:

Dear Partner,

I have changed churches in recent months. You may like this, and you may not, but the important thing is that God commanded me to do it to help bring healing to more people in historic churches as well as to full-gospel groups. I am the same man, only more so . . . a world evangelist called by God to take His healing power to all people of all churches . . . and to win souls!

So began an undated letter which Oral Roberts sent to the people on his mailing list quite sometime after he had joined the Methodist Church in 1968. He did not mention in this particular letter the name of his new denomination or other details of his conversion from Pentecostalism to Methodism other than that it was an order from God. Though leaving the impression throughout this letter that he was continuing his healing ministry and now was planning to carry it to the historic churches, actually it represented another move in Roberts' transition from the type of divine healing practices he had been associated with.

During the 1960s Oral Roberts had been turning to activities other than faith healing. The number of healing campaigns he conducted annually decreased in frequency as well as in the level of emotionalism. By the end of the decade he had divorced himself from faith healing and the extremism characteristic of his early ministry.

While the signs that Oral Roberts was changing had

been visible all along, nevertheless, many of his associates and followers were taken completely by surprise when he left the Pentecostal Holiness Church in favor of the Methodists. They were shocked, feeling insulted and betrayed. They had supported him when he was an unknown, just getting started in his calling. It was through their support that he became famous and continued to prosper. There was a feeling that he was deserting them to assure his own further climb up the social ladder—that they were no longer good enough for him.

The negative reaction that followed was so great that it reportedly almost closed down the ministry of Oral Roberts. Most of his staff was appalled at his decision.[5] I witnessed other deliverance evangelists criticize his conduct. Even many Methodists were dissatisfied with the turn of events. Factions developed within Roberts' enterprises, and he lost many of his supporters. The ministry's income decreased reportedly by more than one third.[6] In retrospect, Roberts commented that, had he known the intensity of opposition to his action, he would have never undertaken this change.[7]

Now it was too late to turn back. But Oral Roberts was not about to give up without a fight. He devised several new methods for increasing his income. He made efforts to win back former supporters and gain new ones. And he succeeded, as once more his resourcefulness saved his ministry from near collapse.

The Formative Years

The formative years and early ministry of Oral Roberts have been recorded in the various editions of his autobiography such as *My Story, My Twenty Years of a Miracle Ministry* and *The Call*. His publications have remained as the only primary sources of much of what occurred during those years.[8,9,10]

That Granville Oral Roberts would become renowned around the entire globe and that his income would reach millions seemed an unlikely possibility in view of the events surrounding his developmental years. Born on Jan. 28, 1918, in Pontotoc County, Okla., he was introduced early in life to the hardships and insecurities of poverty, according to his life stories. Financially, his parents, both natives of Arkansas, were far from comfortable circumstances. They worked hard to make ends meet. Out of the meager income which his father, a tenant farmer turned preacher, struggled to earn, five children had to be provided for, with one of them an incurable epileptic.

Oral, the youngest member of the family, has been described as having been introverted and frail. He was shy with strangers, frequently suffered from illnesses, and stuttered a great deal in his youth. Fights with other children ensued as they tormented him because of his stuttering and ridiculed him for being a "preacher's boy." At home, he received beatings from his father as he and his brother repeatedly engaged in mischief.

Eventually conflicts and personality clashes with other members of his family led to Oral's decision at the age of 16 to run away from home to a nearby town in southern Oklahoma. There he obtained employment as a handyman for a judge, performed other odd jobs, and continued to attend high school. He made a good adjustment in school and, filled with ambition in his new surroundings, dreamed of becoming a lawyer or even the governor of Oklahoma.

About a year after he left home, misfortune suddenly struck Oral. While playing in a basketball tournament, he collapsed, fell to the floor, and blood flowed from his mouth. He was driven home to his family, who began to pray for his recovery. The medical verdict was that Oral apparently had contracted tuberculosis, and he began to fear that he would die.

"My world came crashing down," Roberts recalled in

later years.[11] He stated that it was during this period he came to terms with God and found his Savior in Jesus Christ.

As Oral failed to regain his health, his family decided that his oldest brother should take him to Ada, Okla., where evangelist George Moncey was praying for the sick. At the revival, Brother Moncey prayed over him and commanded the disease to come out of his lungs. Though he felt weak for a while after this meeting, Roberts testified that his stuttering and his tuberculosis were instantly cured. In this story of his faith healing, Roberts also stated that during this trip God spoke to him, stating in an audible voice:

"Son I am going to heal you, and you are to take My healing power to your generation."[12]

Early Ministry

All along Oral Roberts' parents had believed that someday their son would become a highly successful preacher—something his mother had hoped for already before his birth. So it was with parental blessings and encouragement that two months after his supposedly miraculous healing Roberts, now about 18, began to preach the Gospel. He was ordained in the Pentecostal Holiness Church and at first worked with some Bible college students. Then he teamed up with his father, both incorporating prayer for the sick into their ministry.

On Dec. 25, 1938, Oral Roberts married Evelyn Lutman. Of their early years together Evelyn wrote that they started their marriage with borrowed money and were never out of debt for very long. They had to live in other people's homes and did not really know what it was like to have a home of their own.[13] After a while the hardships caused by his calling became difficult to cope with. At one point Evelyn, at the end of her patience, threatened to take the children and leave him.[14]

For 12 years after his entry into the ministry Roberts evangelized, pastored churches, and intermittently took courses from Oklahoma Baptist University and Phillips University. But none of these activities provided him with what he was searching for. He reported that he felt restless, unhappy, and malcontent. Then, in 1947, God allegedly spoke to him again, telling him to be different from other men and to go out and heal the people.[15] Other supernatural signs and messages followed. According to Roberts, it was God's command that he enter deliverance evangelism and heal the sick and cast out the devils.

Roberts, a practical man, reported that he sought out further assurance that this truly was to be his mission in life. He told God that he'd do it—he would resign his pastorate and immediately enter into evangelistic crusades if in return God would provide for his next service, during which he was going to pray for the sick, an audience of 1,000 (he had been preaching to a congregation of around 200), sufficient contributions to cover the costs, and . . . "to heal the people by divine power so conclusively that they, as well as I, would know I was called by God for this special ministry."[16]

According to Roberts, God met all three of his demands. He in turn resigned his pastorate in June 1947, moved his family to Tulsa, and continued holding revival campaigns. He stated that the power of God started to flow like a current of electricity through his "healing" right arm. At times it felt as if a "liquid fire" was surging through his arm; most of the time there was a sensation of warmth.[17]

It was not the gift of healing, however, but rather the confrontation with the gunman that brought him to national attention. The assailant was quickly arrested by the police and told them upon being queried as to his motive for attempting to kill Roberts, "I don't know why I did it."

The man was eventually released by the police. Roberts was now labeled a controversial evangelist, and his revivals prospered greatly from the publicity he received in connection with this incident.

There lay still other "tests of faith" ahead of him. There were times when the audiences did not respond or the attendance was meager. There were challenges and criticisms. On several occasions he became temporarily so discouraged that he wanted to quit.[18]

Though there were setbacks and difficulties, Roberts was gaining proficiency and self-confidence in his calling, and his ministry continued to grow. By the 1950s he had emerged as the most successful of all the deliverance evangelists and was headed for worldwide fame as a faith healer.

Continued Success and Controversy

Through the 1950s his success continued to grow, and testimonies to his healing powers mounted. Antagonism towards him also surfaced occasionally culminating in physical violence. His first television program appeared in 1954, the following year his first live series. These shows brought him many converts as well as strong opposition. Pressure groups started to demand that local television stations take him off the air. They objected primarily to the claimed instant healings occurring at Roberts' touch. In 1959 he was verbally abused, and his cameramen were attacked in an effort to destroy the film he had taken of a synagogue in Capernaum, where Jesus had at one time preached and delivered a man of an unclean spirit. Much to Roberts' consternation, a great deal of speculation and criticism has focused over the years on his personal income, affluent life-style, and his insistence that God's people deserve the best that the world has to offer in material goods.

Unexpectedly virulent opposition to Roberts' ministry

surfaced during his 1956 Australian Crusade. There denouncements against him appeared in the newspapers and rioting broke out at the revival meetings. Hecklers yelled and screamed during the services. Angry crowds defied anyone to accept Christ as their personal Savior. A stink bomb was thrown, one of his trucks was set on fire, and a rope on the big tent was cut. Threats were made to him and Evelyn over the telephone. A frenzied mob tried to rush him, but the police managed to lead him safely from the revival grounds. Then the antagonists booed and tried to overturn a car in which Evelyn was sitting. Opposition became so intense that the crusade had to be canceled, and Roberts and his team flew home to America. Roberts placed much of the blame for these outbursts of hatred and violence on communists, on the bias and sensationalism of the newspaper coverage he received in Australia, and on the reporters' efforts in agitating and supporting the mobs. Many clergymen were also active in the anti-Oral Roberts campaign.

As Oral Roberts became increasingly prosperous and conservative, acceptance and recognition by outsiders grew. He received a kindly welcome from former prime minister of Israel, Ben Gurion. In 1963 he was named "Outstanding American Indian" of the year. He was the guest in the White House of the late president John F. Kennedy and even spoke at the Citadel in Charleston, S.C. Nine years after the riots broke out against him in Australia, he was cordially received back there.

A unique feature about Oral Roberts has been his great success. By 1974 the operating budget of Oral Roberts' enterprises was reported to be about $15,000,000 per year.[19] He had become a guest on talk shows, the star of his own specials on national television, member of the board of trustees of a bank, developer of a retirement community, and president of his own university.

Of the many activities which Oral Roberts has undertaken, the most remarkable accomplishment has been the founding of the Oral Roberts University, a beautiful, ultramodern, fully accredited institution of higher learning. It has a professionally recognized faculty and up-to-date equipment and facilities. The Learning Resources Center on the campus, for example, has been called by the Ford Foundation "one of the most creative facilities on the American campus." In this unusual structure students have access to a highly sophisticated information storage and retrieval system, using the latest in electronic achievement and computer technology.[20] ORU has also received recognition on the collegiate scene for the performance of its basketball team.

Impact of the Deliverance Evangelists

The Oral Roberts University is one of the contributions to have culminated from the efforts of the deliverance evangelists. There have been others. Kathryn Kuhlman, the late president of the Kathryn Kuhlman Foundation, established this nonprofit, charitable religious organization, whose functions were not only to finance her ministry but also to support many welfare activities. It has distributed groceries and other provisions for needy families, has provided scholarships and loans to college students, has aided rehabilitation of the blind and of teenage drug addicts, and has subsidized many missionary churches, schools, and children's homes in remote parts of the world.[21] Somewhat similar activities were engaged in by the Angelus Temple Commissary, founded by Aimee McPherson, which fed and clothed large numbers of impoverished people and provided cash any time day or night for special emergency situations. Sister Aimee was also involved in such endeavors as collecting blood for the Red Cross and selling Liberty Bonds and War Bonds. Her most lasting contribution was the development of a new denomination, the International Church of the Foursquare Gospel, which after her death continued to grow under the leadership of her son, Rolf.[22,23] A number of evangelists have sponsored various halfway houses and children's homes. Knowing from his personal experiences what it is like to be abandoned by parents, Jack Coe built an orphanage for homeless children, which his widow Juanita Coe Hope has been trying to keep going.

A Pentecostal historian, David Harrell, felt that the deliverance evangelists deserve serious study in their own right because of the lasting changes they have produced on religion in America—something that has generally gone unrecognized:

> These men are persistent types of prophets in the Christian tradition—enigmatic and illusive characters in their own day. . .[24]

Harrell has noted that these evangelists have significantly popularized evangelistic missions and faith healing. They promoted ecumenism by urging the Pentecostals to think in undenominational terms. The most prominent individuals among them have stressed the ecumenical nature of their work and emphasized that they want to aid the established full-gospel churches. William Branham has gone on record as labeling denominationalism as the mark of the beast—a stand that alienated many Pentecostal churches.[25]

Harrell viewed the deliverance evangelists as being largely responsible for the unexpected growth of Pentecostalism and having had a definite impact on the emergence of Neo-Pentecostalism, which began to spread in the late 1950s and early 1960s through the traditional churches. As the popularity of Neo-Pentecostalism continued to grow, scores of evangelists began to orient their ministries specifically to attract the followers of this movement. One reason given for Oral Roberts' change of churches was that he came to believe that his strongest backing was coming from sympathizers among the Methodists and other traditional churches.[26]

The deliverance evangelists have further been credited as an important source for the emergence of new sects. The followers of William Branham, some of whom came to think of him almost as God and believed that he would be resurrected after his fatal car accident in 1965, have been observed to be in the early stages of forming a sect. Other evangelists, noticeably the more radical ones with no ties to organized religion, have promoted or established a great many Pentecostal tabernacles and gospel missions which, Harrell predicts, will be bases for future sects.[27]

The Pathfinders

The healing evangelists have traced themselves to Jesus Christ, stating that they wish to recapture the essence of primitive Christianity. They have proclaimed their ministry to be analogous to that of Jesus and that the Bible is their guiding principle. Oral Roberts wrote of his decision to enter the healing ministry:

> What He had done during His earthly ministry and what I felt I should do in my ministry were one and the same—to preach the Gospel and to heal the sick. I wanted my ministry to be against the same four things His was against—sin, demons, disease, and fear. I wanted my ministry to emphasize the same power that His did—the miracle-working power of faith in God.[28]

Many similarities have been recorded between deliverance evangelism and movements such as Montanism that have emerged periodically since the death of the apostles. Yet basically deliverance evangelism can be considered an outgrowth of the American religious experience. It came into its own with the 19th-century

Holiness revivals and the circuit-riding gospel preachers on the frontier and backwoods trails. From these backgrounds came persons who set out to many parts of the land to preach on saving of souls and healing of bodies, thus establishing a tradition for deliverance evangelism. One of them was a man called G. O. Barnes.

G. O. Barnes

G. O Barnes initiated his career in religious work by becoming a missionary to India. Later, back in America, he was in charge of a Presbyterian church until he had serious disagreements with the synod and resigned. He developed an interest in the Plymouth Brethren, but here also a split occurred. Next, Barnes became an assistant to D. L. Moody, the most successful evangelist of his time, who advised him to become one too. At this point Barnes encountered Holiness groups and was converted to the belief that these people possessed the secret of a happier life.

In 1876 Barnes supposedly received the call to preach the Gospel to all men and, giving up his congregation, headed for the mountains of Kentucky.

In the beginning of his evangelistic work, Barnes emphasized the saving of souls only. Later he added the treatment of the sick. He kept a notebook in which he systematically recorded the number saved and the number anointed for healing at each revival. Regarding the origin of his healing ministry, he wrote in his diary:

Visited Mr. and Mrs. Cotton. Both lying in the same bed suffering from neuralgia. I was so moved by the sight of these dear young people thus about to be cut off in the midst of their days that I determined henceforth in the name of the Lord to "obey the Gospel!" and fully carry out my commission, not only to preach the Gospel but "heal the sick," as the Lord gave power, and occasion. The dear Master has been turning my heart in this direction for some time, and in simple reliance on Him alone I will do "what in me lies" to rescue the victims of Satan from his awful clutches.[38]

Besides anointing the sick at his revivals, Barnes also answered requests for prayer that came to him through the mail and visited those who were too sick to leave home. He did refuse to go to see ambulatory cases, insisting that they should acknowledge Christ as the Healer in public.[30]

Testimonies to miraculous cures at his ministry were frequent, involving the usual array of supposedly successful treatments for cancer, nervous conditions, rheumatism, and other diseases. Apparently also reports of failures came to his attention, for he wrote:

I learned last night the secret of apparent failures in bodily healing. It is just as in the soul—some are just saved from hell, some go on to one degree of advancement, and some to another. In body some may be saved from death, who yet are not relieved from aging and suffering and therefore they have received nothing, as the man saved from hell, yet not from temper or drunkenness, seems to have gotten nothing. . . . I cannot tell how this clear teaching gave comfort, in view of so many apparent failures in those who trust the best they can. The degrees are as manifold as in the souls saving. I believe now the weakest faith saves from death, as the weakest of faith saves the soul from perishing.[31]

Barnes believed that all disease as well as medicine and herbs were the work of the devil, and so, when illness was about to strike him, he would place all his trust in the Lord and avoid the medical profession. He was going to have quite a struggle keeping his faith as health problems plagued him throughout life.

As his reputation grew, he extended his revivals from rural Kentucky to cities where he visited faith cure homes and worked with sympathetic ministers, both Negro and Caucasian. In 1882 Barnes met with the well-known faith healer A. B. Simpson, the founder of one of the largest Holiness sects, and assisted him in one of his consecration and healing meetings.[32]

John Alexander Dowie

Before the turn of the century the most successful of all the healers hitherto, John Alexander Dowie, was fast becoming a household word in this country and even beginning to attract attention in Europe. Having emigrated from Australia, he was not a product of American revivalism. But many of his followers were, having flocked to him from the Holiness movement and similar sects and cults that had come into existence before Dowie's arrival in the United States.

Seeking a friendlier and more fertile environment in which to expand his healing ministry, he migrated in 1888 to America, receiving a warm welcome when he arrived at San Francisco, where stories of his activities had been circulating for some time. Five years later he moved to Chicago, where no more than a year after his arrival the sick and disabled were pursuing him in such droves that he leased three hotels and turned them into faith cure homes. In these homes the patients were taught to disregard all medical treatment, even for communicable disease and broken bones, both of which, they were told, were just as susceptible to divine healing as the maladies that might be of a more psychosomatic nature. Dowie was especially against medication, druggists, and physicians, seeing them all as the direct inspiration of the devil.[33] Instead, he argued, one was to use God for his healing. When asked about the undeniable failures of faith cures for some of the sick persons, he replied that no one can be cured without faith, and the fact that illness lingers proves that the patient does not have enough faith—if he wants to get well he must learn to believe.[34]

However, some patients did not respond to the treatment methods prescribed by Dowie, and several deaths occurred in these homes. The city authorities, alarmed at the possible consequences if people continued to be attracted to Dowie's philosophy on health and happiness, initiated an investigation of him and in 1895 charged him, among other things, with manslaughter, neglect, and practicing medicine without a license. The higher courts, however, held the city ordinances that Dowie violated as unconstitutional, and in the end Dowie emerged as the victor in his struggle with the municipal authorities.[35]

In 1899 Dowie announced the founding of the Christian Catholic Church of Zion and declared himself to be a messenger of God. By 1901 he was claiming to be the reincarnation of Elijah with a mission to prepare the earth for the return of Christ.[36] That year Dowie's vision of utopian communal community also became a reality with the founding of Zion City some 40 miles north of Chicago.

For some time Dowie enjoyed tremendous success and popularity. Then fate seemed to have turned against him. The first major misfortune occurred one morning when his daughter, Esther, was seriously burned as a breeze blew her nightgown into a lit lamp. Dowie hurried to her side and found that one of his followers, who, oddly enough, was also a physician, had tried to ease her pain with vaseline. After banishing the physician from the Christian Catholic Church of Zion for using such a pagan technique, Dowie prayed by Esther's side all day and refused to allow any medical treatment. In the evening she died in agony. In an attempt to save face, Dowie explained that she died because she had ignored his injuction against employing alcohol in any form. It seemed that Esther had used alcohol in the lamp whose flames had burned her.[37] His callous reaction to this tragedy did not endear him to the public, and opposition to him grew even among those who had previously tended to lean favorably towards his teachings.

Other scandals, setbacks, and misfortunes followed. His costly New York City healing-revival campaign was sabotaged, he was accused of sexual irregularities, his family rejected him, he suffered from a stroke, Zion City was declared bankrupt, and other problems beset him. There seemed nothing else for him to do other than to withdraw from all activities he had engaged in before, and in a state of depression and total discouragement he lay in bed for six months till his death in March 1907, leaving behind confused believers and a troubled community of some 6,000.

Many who were influenced by Dowie, whether or not they settled in Zion City, became involved after his death with the Holiness, Full Gospel, or Pentecostal groups. Some of the more prominent leaders in faith healing, such as F. F. and B. B. Bosworth, John G. Lake, Dr. Phineas Youkum, and Raymond T. Richey, emerged from this setting and have left their imprint on deliverance evangelism.[38] To Harrell, it is John Alexander Dowie who is the father of healing evangelism.[39]

The Pentecostal Movement

Pentecostalism encompasses a great variety of fundamentalist or evangelical cults, sects, and denominations that are primarily concerned with perfection, holiness, the literal acceptance of the Bible, and a renewal of the Pentecostal experience. Its members believe that the nine gifts of the Holy Spirit—knowldege, wisdom, faith, divine healing, discerning spirits, speaking in tongues, interpretation of tongues, prophecy, and working miracles—are to be found in Christian churches today just as in the past. Many of them have emphasized especially the gift of tongues, which is considered the sign of baptism by the Holy Spirit.[40,41] For faith healing, this movement was to have major ramifications.

While many have viewed Pentecostalism as an extension of the Holiness movement, more frequently it has been traced to Charles F. Parham and the events of 1901 or to William J. Seymour and the Azusa Street revivals.

The Early Days   Charles F. Parham (1873–1929) was the chief leader of this movement during the 1901–06 period, and the first Pentecostal witnesses who went out preaching had been his students.

His first religious affiliation was with the Congregational Church, where already at the tender age of 15 he served in the capacity of a lay preacher. Later Parham became associated with the Methodists, from whose ranks he withdrew to join the rapidly expanding Holiness movement.[42]

When he was 16 he began to have doubts about entering the ministry and seemed to have lost all interest in the church. While in this frame of mind, he was stricken with rheumatic fever. He failed to respond to treatment and ultimately became so ill that little hope was held for his life. He started to believe that his physical condition was caused by his rebellion against God, and consequently he reconsecrated his life to God and decided to enter the ministry if only he would recover. Years afterward he testified that with this rededication every joint in his body loosened and every organ was healed, and to this incident he later attributed his becoming a proponent of faith healing.[43]

Inspired by Dowie's example, Parham opened the Bethel Healing Home in Topeka, Kans., in 1898. This type of home, which seemed to have been rather popular at that time, sought to provide appropriate surroundings for infirm persons who wanted to retreat to a place where they could be helped by faith healing. These homes were called faith homes not only because of the healing aspect but also because in many cases no charge was made for services; they operated on faith that God would provide all material requirements through gifts of concerned, magnanimous Christians.[44]

In 1900 Parham opened the Bethel Bible School, where in 1901 the speaking in tongues movement erupted. According to Nichols, though sporadic outbreaks of glossolalia have appeared throughout history, it was here that for the first time the concept of being baptized or filled with the Holy Ghost was linked to just one outward sign—speaking in tongues.[45]

Initially the Parhamites were not successful. The great excitement among his followers in response to the appearance of glossolalia at his Bible college in Topeka, Kans., was followed by two years of hardships and frustrations as the early revival efforts failed to popularize the new faith and attract converts. Severe criticisms were launched against them by the newspapers and established churches, and they often encountered discriminatory practices specially directed against them. Many buildings were closed to them, and proprietors refused to rent them their facilities. Parham often found himself preaching in the streets, where verbal abuses by the irate populace flowed freely.

In August 1903 Parham was preaching on divine healing in Eldorado Springs, Mo. Afterward two persons claimed to have been cured of their ills. While many considered him a neurotic, others began to respond favorably to his exhortations. When he went on to Galena, increasingly larger crowds started to fill his tent as news of supposedly miraculous happenings spread. The *Cincinnati Inquirer,* dated Jan. 27, 1904, reported:

> Almost three months have elapsed since this man
> came to Galena, and during that time he has healed
> over a thousand people and converted more than

800. . . . Here people who have not walked for years without the aid of crutches have risen from the altar with their limbs so straightened that they were enabled to lay aside their crutches. . . . These cures . . . are effected solely through prayer and faith. Nothing else is done, though Mr. Parham often lays his hands on the afflicted one.[46]

One of the many students of Parham who set out on their own to spread the Gospel was William J. Seymour, a Negro Holiness preacher. It was he who developed into the major Pentecostal leader in California and one of the most important pioneers of the movements.

On April 9, 1906, Seymour's followers (an integrated group composed mostly of whites), having been in prayer for several days, began to break into ecstatic utterances which were interpreted as the apostolic tongues. These meetings continued almost without stopping for over three months, during which time the occurences of miraculous healings were reported. The press coverage of these meetings was highly antagonistic. This, however, promoted its growth; many who came to scoff found themselves converted. From Los Angeles this movement expanded across the United States and by 1908 had spread to other countries.

Aimee McPherson Of the many deliverance evangelists that came out of the Pentecostal movement, Aimee Semple McPherson was one to receive worldwide renown; her escapades were to fill the front pages for several decades.

The child of a onetime Salvation Army lassie and a Methodist farmer, Aimee was dedicated to the Lord's service in a Salvation Army barrack by her mother. After a period of religious skepticism in her teens, Aimee was converted in 1907 at the age of 17 to Pentecostalism by an itinerate preacher, Robert Semple, whom she married shortly thereafter. Semple died in China, where the young couple had gone as missionaries, leaving Aimee alone and penniless with an infant daughter, Roberta.

Back in the United States, Aimee married Harold McPherson, a grocery salesman, in 1912, and they had a son, Rolf. Her second husband, after earnest efforts, failed to get enthusiastic about the "old-time religion" and complained about Aimee's hysterical behavior and her neglect and abuse of him. After five years the marriage ended in divorce.

Eventually Aimee managed to save enough money to buy an old tent and continued her travels from coast to coast. She preached to the poor and the "backward," and often faced hardships of many kinds—hunger, natural disasters, overwork and the jeers of hostile mobs.

After years of attracting a meager attendance to her revivals and having only a sparse following, her persistence finally paid off. In 1921, in San Diego, she enjoyed her first successful revival. Largely because of the miraculous healings which were claimed to have occurred there, other well-attended meetings ensued. Her popularity was further enhanced by the publicity given to several near-riots among the multitudes of sufferers who clamored for her healing touch. In San Diego the demand for her ministration became so great that the authorities turned over Balboa Park for her use. There she reportedly anointed and prayed for the sick as they passed before her for two days from morning till night, until she fainted from exhaustion.[47] On the heels of this campaign many more triumphs followed as she traveled on to other cities.

Los Angeles was the place where she eventually chose to settle down, and there she soon amassed a sizable fortune. Four years after her arrival she built the huge Angelus Temple that was to replace the tent and sawdust as the major locale for her services and the host of other activities that she sponsored. Though she seemed to seek out scandals and intrigues and engaged in behavior in direct contradiction of her teachings, the devotion of her followers never slackened.

Growth of the Movement   Since its beginnings at Bethel Bible School in Topeka, Kans., modern Pentecostalism has been expanding rapidly across the world. Originally it was meant to be a movement within the various denominations. However, before long many believers found themselves expelled from their churches or highly ridiculed and consequently formed their own religious bodies, such as the Assemblies of God.

During the 1960s and 1970s the Pentecostal groups were experiencing a noticeable growth and were encompassing an increasingly broader section of Americans. The Assemblies of God, for example, grew from 515,000 members in 1963 to 625,000 in 1970—this at a time when some of the major "liberal" denominations were faced with stagnation or decline in membership. As a denomination they have also been successful overseas, particularly in Brazil where some two million members point up a growth rate of 10 percent per year.[48]

According to the *U. S. News and World Report:*

> Now it's a wave of old-time . . . religion that is gaining converts across America. . . . What is developing in some ways is a replay of an earlier era when tent-meeting evangelism brought unbelievers down "the sawdust trail" and imported faiths, such as theosophy, drew earnest seekers after truth.[49]

Though appealing generally to a different segment of the population than Pentecostalism, a related movement, Neo-Pentecostalism or the charismatic movement, emerged between 1956 and 1960. Neo-Pentecostalism spread among many denominations belonging to the World Council of Churches, including Episcopalians, Lutherans, and Methodists. By 1967 it had reached the Roman Catholic Church; other religious bodies were also affected by it.

In spite of repeated attacks by those outside its ranks over such practices as speaking in tongues, Neo-Pentecostalism has continued to grow at a rapid pace. In 1975 the number of followers was estimated to be between 500,000 and one million. However, by the mid-1970s it also faced bitter conflicts that posed a truly serious threat to it, particularly in reference to "discipleship" or "shepherding."[50] Dr. Martin E. Marty was reported to have stated that Neo-Pentecostalism had peaked by 1976. Indications were that stagnation or downward trends could be expected thereafter for Neo-Pentecostalism and the various off-beat religious movements that had mushroomed during the previous decade.[51]

Healing Revivals of the 20th Century

Pre-World War II Days   Many who set out in the early years of the 20th century to hold deliverance revivals were inspired by the Azusa Street Mission meetings. In addition to them, some of the more or less established evangelists, like Mary Woodworth Etter, who had been preaching healing since 1876, were starting to attract growing audiences as Pentecostalism gained an increasing hold on the souls of Americans.[52]

By the 1920s several British evangelists, notably Smith Wigglesworth and Charles S. Price, were touring the country, and a number of American evangelists had established independent ministries. The most successful of them remained Aimee McPherson, but others were also attracting large followings.

Then came the depression, and the large healing campaign became a rarity because of financial difficulties. The touring ministries of Aimee McPherson and F. F. Bosworth gradually tapered off. Raymond T. Richey was forced to leave the field and became a pastor. It was not until 1951 that he once again became a full-time evangelist. Other popular evangelists likewise fell upon hard times.[53]

According to Lindsay, evangelism was kept alive mainly by dedicated ministers who went from church to church preaching the Gospel and accepting such opportunities as opened to them, often receiving no financial remuneration. It was not uncommon, according to Lindsay, for offerings to amount to less than a dollar, and receiving as much as $20 was infrequent.[54]

During this period there appeared what might be called "hobo evangelists," who rode the rails in the manner of the sons of the road, sleeping in flop houses and eating at missions as they sought opportunities for preaching. Lindsay stated that there were dedicated individuals among them, but a number were shiftless and ignorant and on arrival in a town expected to be put up and fed, yet were completely unprepared for the ministry. Some of them were actually nothing more than tramps who seemed to be proud of their escapades as they roamed the countryside.[55]

The Revival Explosion The emerging postwar revivals have been viewed by Harrell as overshadowing the successes of the evangelists. This great resurgence in the popularity of deliverance evangelism, which started in 1946–47, has been credited by many to the ministry of William Marrion Branham, an ordained independent Baptist minister born in the hills of Kentucky. As a consequence of his preaching and praying for the sick in his St. Louis campaigns, his reputation began to grow among select Pentecostal groups. Next he was invited by "Dad" Humbard, the father of Rex Humbard, to hold revivals in Jonesboro, Ark. There huge crowds came to hear him, and reports were circulated that he had raised a man from the dead. Harrell stated:

39

Branham had struck into the heartland of fervent pentecostalism—a heartland starved for a message of old-time miracle power.[56]

Other successful revivals followed him in his travels across the country, and the Pentecostal community was increasingly hearing about a new miracle worker.

Many started to come to Branham's revivals to emulate his techniques. Others came to observe and became inspired to set out also on the gospel circuit. A few of those who were influenced by this man, who claimed to have been commanded by an angel to bring healing to the sick, were Oral Roberts, T. L. Osborn, O. L. Jaggers, Gayle Jackson, and Gordon Lindsay.

Gordon Lindsay, an Assemblies of God minister, born in Zion City, where his parents were disciples of John Alexander Dowie, had experienced conversion to Pentecostalism from his contact with Charles F. Parham. Much of Lindsay's career had been that of an evangelist, and for a short period he had also been a Foursquare Gospel minister. Upon observing Branham he decided to resign from his pastorate and become his manager.

As many men and women, often from poverty-stricken Pentecostal churches, rushed into this field, Lindsay set out to organize them and publicize their ministries. In 1949 Lindsay arranged in Dallas the first convention of deliverance evangelists. The next year about 1,000 evangelists met in Kansas City. Almost all of the important figures, except Branham and Roberts, attended it.

Following the spectacular expansion of this movement during the next years (1947–52), Harrell saw four very serious obstacles appearing in the paths of the evangelists: one was that they were misunderstood and caricatured by the press; another was the opposition from the medical profession; a third one was rejection by most other Christian groups; and finally ostracism by the major Pentecostal churches. These proved fatal for not just a few evangelistic enterprises.[57]

The heyday for the evangelists was over by 1958. Many were forced out of the field, others had to make drastic changes and come up with innovations. The major cause of all this was, according to Harrell, loss of financial contributions as a result of the opposition by the Pentecostal churches. Some additional causes for their difficulties were that the field had become oversaturated with evangelists, "miracles" were becoming too commonplace and their claims too unbelievable, and many sincere participants became appalled at the successes of frauds and extremists.[58]

Decline and Reorganization As support from the Pentecostal churches waned, the evangelists began to search for new sources of followers. Overseas crusades continued to be a lucrative business, and an increasing number of evangelists started to emphasize foreign missions. In this country members of traditional churches became interested in the Neo-Pentecostal movement, and so a number of the evangelists started to attract these people. Frequently the evangelists switched to overseas missionary or benevolent societies and held healing revivals on those occasions they found convenient.[59]

Gordon Lindsay started to involve himself largely with missionary work and withdrew from the activities of the deliverance evangelists. Consequently W. V. Grant began in the early 1960s to take over more and more as the organizer and publicist for the movement. The Full Gospel Business Men's Fellowship International came to aid the evangelists financially and with business advice. In turn many evangelists became unofficial promoters of new chapters during their campaigns.[60]

This period also witnessed growing internal dissension and self-appraisal from within the ranks of the evangelists. There were concerns with frauds, exploitation, and

41

other unethical conduct on the part of their colleagues. By the mid-1960s the evangelists were no longer a group. Healing revivals had become, in the words of one of them, "a lonely business."[61] At the close of the 1960s with Oral Roberts having withdrawn from faith healing, the two evangelists who came to the forefront were the radical and controversial A. A. Allen and the widely respected Kathryn Kuhlman, representing the two extremes of deliverance evangelism.

The 1970's By 1975 the old-time deliverance evangelism was reported to have at least partially recovered from the previous decline. Numerous tent revivals were being conducted across the nation. Many of the same doctrines were preached as during the 1950s and respectable sized crowds were attracted to this form of ministry. Scores of the more moderate participants, however, complained that the typical revivals of the 1970s had retained the form but not much of the spirit of the earlier campaigns. Harrell observed that the revivals, with a few notable exceptions, came to be modeled after the ministry of A. A. Allen. Allen himself died in 1970, cutting short a spectacularly successful career. He left a legacy notably in such evangelists as Leroy Jenkins, Robert Schambach, and Don Stewart.[62]

Harrell observed that the deliverance evangelists of the 1970s, in contrast to those of earlier times, were more boisterous and made more extreme claims regarding their gift of miracles; the former ecumenical fervor was replaced by harsh anti-institutionalism; greater high pressure tactics were used in obtaining donations; doctrines other than healing gained ascendancy, particularly the prosperity doctrine with its promises of financial miracles; and a greater diversity in styles, more staged and professional performances, and a loss of spontaneity came to characterize the revivals of this period.[63]

Since many of those that had been active in the field

during the post-world war II period had withdrawn or partially retired by the end of the 1960s, their places were being taken by a number of talented young preachers who, according to Harrell, brought new vitality to the revival scene. To Harrell, the most outstanding of the newcomers was Jimmy Swaggart, an Assemblies of God minister and one of the nation's top gospel singers. He was the first deliverance evangelist since the early 1950s to receive the enthusiastic backing of the Assemblies of God.[64]

Though some discrimination and prejudice towards the deliverance evangelists continued to exist, Harrell observed that those familiar with the healing revivals of the 1950s could hardly have guessed that the deliverance evangelists could ever attain the respectability they came to command two decades later.[65]

One person who could be credited in part for the increased respectability of deliverance evangelism in the eyes of the American people was Kathryn Kuhlman. Kuhlman managed to obtain respect and admiration even from a large segment of the population who held religious viewpoints vastly different from hers. The ranks of those who have praised her have included physicians, clergymen, and civic leaders. In 1967, she was awarded the keys to the city of Pittsburgh to commemorate the 20th anniversary of her ministry there.[66] When she was in Rome, she received an invitation to visit the Pope.[67]

Kuhlman emerged as by far the most successful of all the faith healers of the mid 1970s. Her ministry was bringing in $2 to 3 million annually, and an estimated 2 million persons have claimed healing through her ministry since 1946.[68] She held services also in other parts of the country. Devoting much time to Southern California, she filled the 7,000 seat Shrine Auditorium in Los Angeles to overflowing each month.[69]

Suddenly on Dec. 27, 1975, she was hospitalized in Tulsa and the following day underwent open-heart surgery. The doctors were reportedly optimistic about her recovery. When asked whether faith healing had been sought for her, D. B. Wilkerson, a Tulsa car dealer and personal adviser replied,

"God didn't elect to give her a miracle that way."[70]

The year 1975 had been a fateful year for her. Before this surgery she had been hospitalized twice, reportedly for minor heart flare-ups.[71] Things were published about her personal life and ministry that had upset her greatly. Dr. William Nolen had attacked her involvement in healing. She was sued by her former television agent and settled out of court. There was a break with her popular pianist, Dino, because, among other reasons, she opposed his choice of spouse. Both of these men suggested that the evangelist's personal life was quite different from her public image.[72] Allegations were made as to her use of alcoholic beverages and misuse of funds.[73] Kuhlman became convinced that they were opportunists trying to wreck her ministry.[74] All this may well have had a critical impact on her physical health.

Although she did recover successfully from the surgery, she failed to regain her strength.[75] Besides her friend Wilkerson, the only other visitor she permitted to see her was Oral Roberts.[76] On Feb. 20, 1976, she died of pulmonary hypertension.[77] Russell Chandler of the *Los Angeles Times* wrote:

> During those last months, even as illness and criticism cast shadows, Miss Kuhlman's fame continued to grow. She was still on the rise as a widely loved and acclaimed religious figure.[78]

Following Kuhlman's death, bitter conflict erupted between her staff and Wilkerson over her newly drafted will. There were also speculations as to who would come to fill the "vacuum" left by her demise. Some predicted the emergence of a yet unknown figure, while evangelists. Roxanne Brant was one of those considered to eventually succeed her. Young, attractive, well-educated, Brant has been carrying a taxing revival schedule. She reported that during 1975 year she held 54 different crusades totaling 224 miracle services, during which 15,680 ailing persons were healed. In 1976 her ministry to Latin America expanded as she held mass healing campaigns and sponsored native churches and evangelists:

"The Lord has spoken to me and told me to go to South America . . . and . . . preach the gospel of Jesus Christ with power and signs following."

others suggested names from among the established

Chapter 3

Becoming a Faith Healer

She sat the three-year-old in a tiny club chair with a flowered print slip cover. He squirmed for a moment until he nestled obediently into the seat. Then he stared at his hands, which he kept clasped in his lap. She gently lifted his chin with her hand until their eyes were level. The intensity of her gaze warned him that what was happening was important.

Seated across from him she began reading aloud a four-minute sermon. Then she explained the Bible verses it was based on, and asked him if he understood. He shook his head. She read the sermon again, repeating each line over and over. Then he repeated each line after her, not in his natural voice, but in a chesty roar, imitating her perfect diction. In twenty minutes his attention lagged.

Lifting him by the seat of his pants she took him to the kitchen sink and let cold water run over his head. He was gasping for breath when she turned off the tap, dried him, and put him back in his little chair. The reading-repeating session began again. In a half hour his gaze wandered. She lifted him again, took him to the sofa, and held a pillow over his face until he begged to go back to his chair. After the first day, punishments were no longer necessary, and she trained him five hours a day for four weeks. Finally the child had perfectly memorized his first sermon.[79]

47

This is how Marjoe Gortner became an evangelist, according to his biographer, Steven S. Gaines. Gaines revealed that it was no divine inspiration but rather an ambitious mother, with desire for an evangelist's career for herself, who manipulated Marjoe's entry into the revival ministry. Being a young child, Marjoe really did not have any choice in the decision. But what about others who enter this field? What kind of persons would set out on the gospel circuit to try to save souls and heal the sick? Is there something unique about their background and personality that would propel them to become deliverance evangelists?

In my investigation to answer these questions, I was able to obtain through various revival magazines, interviews with knowledgeable people, and other sources the names of 164 deliverance evangelists. Follow-up revealed that a number of them had died, retired, left the country, or simply dropped out of sight. I was able to locate 78 of them and compiled biographical sketches of varying degrees of completeness for 60 in regards to their life before the deliverance evangelism ministry.[80] These 60 I tried to follow up over an extended period of time (during which I also came across life stories of a few additional evangelists) to obtain more information or to verify those previously collected.

My main sources for information on their backgrounds were the many life stories that have been written by the evangelists themselves and/or their supporters, critics, or simply neutral observers. The life stories ranged from full-length books to illustrated pamphlets to articles in obscure mimeographed journals. These sources I supplemented with information provided by *McCalls Magazine, Newsweek, Reader's Digest, Time,* and many other magazines and newspapers, as well as by interviews and special files, such as those of the Milwaukee Better Business Bureau.

In their own colorful jargon, with possibly more than just a little embellishment, the evangelists have narrated stories of personal hardships and psychic experiences. From my own investigation, I find generally no reason to question the truthfulness of their statements regarding such data as their place of birth, number of siblings, and occupation of their father. However, skeptics have not been willing to accept their claims to supernatural contacts, an area on which only the evangelists can give the answers, and proof remains beyond easy verification. Yet even if their claims are to be construed as false, they nevertheless provide clues to their personality and the kind of image they feel necessary to project in order to succeed in their ministry.

Pool of Recruitment:
The Place of Birth

The geographical areas which have spawned a disproportionately large number of deliverance evangelists are the rural areas and small towns of the West South Central region of the United States. Fifty-three percent of the evangelists were born in rural areas and another 34 percent in villages or small towns. Only 13 percent were from medium or large-sized cities (population 100,000 or more). Thirty-three percent were born in either Texas or Oklahoma, with those of Southern origin comprising 63 percent of the sample. In contrast, no one in the sample was born in any of the New England states.

That the rural areas and small towns of the South have been supplying a larger number of evangelists than the other regions of the country may be explained partially by the religious tradition prevailing there. During the previous century the population of the Southern states was widely scattered. This has meant, according to Thomas Sowell, that providing services, including religious ones, has been costly in both time and money. Thus, out of expediency, sporadic visits by itinerant preachers replaced regular church services. This tended to produce an emotional revival-style religion suited to occasional redemption rather than a day-to-day ministry.[81] Though conditions in these communities have changed, aspects of the revival have survived and exposure of Holiness and Pentecostal forms of worship have continued to be more prevalent than in the North.[82,83] At the same time, opportunities to get ahead in these communities, as in similar ones elsewhere, have been limited, and few chances exist for the young to be closely exposed to a diversity of occupations that they could realistically hope to enter. All this has contributed to the attractiveness of evangelism as an occupational choice.

Socio-Economic Background

The day-to-day existence of the family of the evangelists in their early years was often characterized by economic hardships and material want. Seventy-one percent of the evangelists grew up in lower-class homes, less than a third (29%) in working or middle-class and none in upper-middle- or upper-class homes. Many of them experienced during their early childhood the impact of the prairie state dust storms and the great depression, both of which fell with a special severity on the least affluent segment of the population. Even those who were fortunate enough to have escaped the hardships of these periods were likely to have been exposed to a life of poverty during their formative years.

M.M. Baker recalled his childhood: "I was born in a very small town by the name of Belton, Texas. . . . My parents were very poor. We were so poor the poor people called us poor. . . . To get to our house in the country, one would have to turn off the main road onto a little dirt road; then to a little lane. . . . We didn't have electricity. . . . We didn't have running water in the house. . . . When my mother would wash, she would wash out in the back yard in one of these old iron washpots. She put the clothes in the washpot, built a fire under the washpot, and let the clothes soak there. . . . I know what it is to sit down at the table with nothing to eat except corn meal mush, or gravy thickened with just water and a little meal."[84]

Little David stated: "When I was 7 years of age, we moved to Cudahy, Wisconsin. Our family was very poor, and we lived in a one-room filling station, which had been converted into a house. It had a cement floor that always seemed to leak water from nowhere. I remember the terrible winters we spent there in that damp place with only one small burner to keep us warm. . . . But regardless of how hard Dad tried it seemed as though this was the best he could do for the family."[85]

Just how much poverty they have had to endure and how many difficulties they have had to overcome is repeatedly told by the evangelists at the revival meetings and recorded in their life stories. These narrations, real or exaggerated, no doubt appeal to many of the poorer people who themselves have had experiences with similar situations. Though their teachings tend to emphasize that it is better to be rich than poor, the evangelists, over-all, have claimed that their disadvantaged background has aided them in coping with the problems of life and in doing God's work. According to William Branham:

"Rarely have those who have received an unusual calling from God been reared in homes of the rich, or have come from aristocratic families. The Savior Himself was cradled in a manger. . . . Humility and sturdiness of character are developed best amid the rugged life that comes from hardships and sometimes suffering and poverty."[86]

In some cases the cause of their poverty was a father who was absent or negligent. Not too infrequently much of the badly needed income went to support the father's drinking and gambling. Velmer Garner tells of the days before his father was saved:

"All through my life I hated liquor. I saw what it did to my father. He would cry and say he would never drink again, but it was the same old story. His pay check would be gone on drinking and gambling. He was bound by the power of the devil. I never had any toys or bicycles, because everything my daddy could get he would spend it on liquor."[87]

More common causes of their poverty were, however, the hard times and lack of the right kind of occupational skills. Many of their parents found themselves struggling at jobs that were financially unrewarding. Thus they could provide only a sparse living to their families, some of which consisted of as many as 14 children.

The most common occupation of the father was farming. In nearly half (44%) of the families the father either owned a small farm, was a tenant farmer, or was employed as a farm laborer. It was hard work and required the help of the rest of the family, including the small children. The second most frequent occupation of the father was some sort of a religious vocation, usually a preacher. In more than a third (35%) of the families the father was a minister, evangelist, missionary, or combination preacher-farmer or preacher-laborer. Here too the family often worked together as a unit, with the mother possibly playing the organ and the children singing gospel songs. In the rest of the families the father was primarily an unskilled or semi-skilled worker (16%) or a small businessman (6%).

One reason why deliverance evangelism is more attractive to persons of lower-class backgrounds is that this form of religious expression has been more familiar to and compatible with them than with the higher classes. Studies have shown that though individuals from the lower classes are less active in religious affairs (a reversal of this particular pattern has been observed for the South by Reed[88]), when they do become involved, they are more likely to affiliate with highly fundamentalist and emotional groups.[89] Also for the lower classes deliverance evangelism would provide a means of upward mobility. In contrast, middle- and upper-class parents are likely to look with great disfavor on this field as a career choice for their children.

Family Relations

During their formative years the lives of the deliverance evangelists were jarred not only by the uncertainties and struggles of their family to maintain their meager subsistence but also by their frequent change of place of residence or conflicts between parents.

In homes where the father was involved with a religious vocation the family might have been kept moving from one community to another as the father preached the Word of God. Contributions were often meager, and a gift of food from some kindly parishioner saved the family on many a night from going to bed hungry. The father appeared as a stern disciplinarian and rigid in his outlook. The family life as a rule was stable and orderly, and the parents worked together as a unit for a common cause.

Charles Young wrote: "I can never remember a Sunday I didn't go to church. In fact I remember very few nights I wasn't in church. I spent a lot of my early life traveling with my parents in the evangelistic field. . . . While we were in revivals, we . . . generally stayed with the pastor or some of the saints. . . . I sang every night in my father's revivals. Mom would stand me on the pulpit or altar bench, I would sing several songs a night. I begin singing tenor with the family when I was five."[90]

As many as one third of them, however, grew up in homes broken by divorce, desertion, separation, or death. Several were reared by grandparents, and three of them spent part of their childhood in an orphanage, where they were left by parents who were either unwilling or unable to care for them. In many other cases, though the parents managed to stay together, hostilities and fights were frequent. If there was a stepfather at home, conflict seemed even more common.

A. A. Allen described life with his new stepfather, John:

"Mother would swear like a sailor, and the least of the curses and insults she hurled at John was, 'You lousy nigger!' . . . Many times my sisters and I heard them cursing, swearing, and battling all night long. Many times Mother and John slapped each other around. Occasionally, Mother would take out her .38 and threaten to shoot John. . . . John had a gun, too, an angry-looking .45. When he had endured all he thought he could take, he would pull it out and declare he was going to kill Mother, all us kids, and himself. . . . Their quarrels would invariably be patched up in a day or so, only to be shortly resumed no more than a week later."[91]

Whether the father was a dedicated preacher who spent his free time with the family or a rootless laborer who was usually out "living it up," the young future evangelists tended to be at least somewhat estranged, if not outright hostile, towards him. With a few notable exceptions, the relationship between them appeared strained and lacking in overt affection. The father was frequently pictured as a strict disciplinarian, easily provoked to give a whipping, and rigid in his outlook. In addition, a number of fathers were criticized for excessive drinking, gambling, neglect of family, and "backsliding" in general. Ralph Hart recalled:

> As time passed and we moved from town to town, there was one thing we learned. Daddy always laid down rules for us to live by, and we knew we'd better follow them to the letter, or else we'd end up in the woodshed with a very sore sittin' down place. Daddy believed that a pat on the back hard enough and low enough would make a believer out of any child. He taught us with a razor strap in one hand and a Bible in the other. The combination was mighty convincing. He raised six boys. Five of them are preachers today.[92]

In contrast to alienation from their father most evangelists stated that they had a very close relationship with their mother. With the exception of two, who referred to their mother in such terms as "immoral" and "plain no-good," they usually praised her highly. In a few other instances where they did mention certain questionable behavior on her part, they were quick to offer rationalizations.

From the evangelists' possibly romanticized descriptions, the typical mother appeared to be a pious, serious, quiet spoken, but firm woman who loved her children and worried about the family's spiritual and financial welfare. She was busy with her children and chores—working in the fields alongside her husband, aiding him in his religious calling, or supplementing the family income by taking in ironing and wash. She was seen as the more practical, stable, and compassionate parent. Whenever disagreements arose at home, the evangelists were more likely to side with her than with the father. Don Stewart stated:

> Growing up as the baby of the family, I was the closest to my mother, the most distant of the children from my dad. Mom stayed home and spent all her time outside church shepherding her rambunctious flock of six

kids. . . . My initial display of temper in public occurred the first day I was shuffled off to kindergarten. Separation from my mother was so traumatic that I cried loud and lustily. . . . I was mama's boy and couldn't bear the thought of being away from her.[98]

Many of the evangelists have recalled that it was their parents and kin, especially the mothers, who had encouraged them already early in life to choose a religious vocation. The significance of this for their future decision is supported by research findings demonstrating that people are strongly influenced by the advice of their family and friends when they select an occupation.

Peer Group

By today's standards the evangelists, on the average, grew up in relatively large families. In the sample I investigated the number of brothers and sisters ranged from 1 to 13. Approximately one third (34%) had six or more siblings.

Several of the evangelists indicated in their life stories that they had to rely in their childhood primarily on their brothers for companionship. They apparently were not able to cultivate as intense and long-lasting friendships with other children as their peers because of discrimination against Pentecostals, their low status in the community, the many time-consuming chores assigned to them and, most of all, because their family moved so frequently from one place to another. There were occasions when other children laughed at their shabby clothes, made fun of their parents' religion, contemptuously called them "preacher's boy," and threw stones at them, in this and other ways precipitating quarrels and fistfights. Of growing up in the small towns of Arizona, Don Steward wrote:

Cottonwood, Clarkdale, and Jerome . . . had no more than 5,000 people, and Pentecostals were not only a minority, but the object of scorn and derision. Most of the kids I knew in school were Mexicans and Catholic. The first curse words I learned were in Spanish. As I grew up, I was called a Holy Roller so often I began to be ashamed of my church and the way we worshiped. My only explanation was that we were just about like the Baptists, only we prayed louder. Because we were soldered so tightly to the rules of our faith, I found I had little in common with the other kids I knew. I could participate in a few of their activities. . . . We couldn't read comic books, go to the movies, and dancing outside the church wasn't permitted. On the radio we couldn't listen to what my folks called 'worldly' music—jazz or swing. My sisters couldn't wear slacks or makeup.[94]

Alongside the bleak memories of being rejected, the evangelists also reported the good times they enjoyed—of the fun they had romping around the fields or playing games with the other children. The one game many of them have later recollected was playing church in imitation of their elders. Leroy Jenkins stated that already as a child he loved to play the part of the preacher. At times when he was unable to persuade other children to play his congregation, he would climb a tree and preach to the birds.

While mother worked, Polly took care of us. We often gathered the neighbor children together and played church. I would be the preacher. We used boxes for a pulpit and a large kitchen spoon for a mike. We sang some off-key songs, and I told the kids they were all a bunch of reprobates and were on their way to hell. This caused some of the children to cry. One day our pet cat died. We gathered together for the funeral. . . . I told the children if they would agree in prayer for the cat it would return to life. We all laid our hands on the cat and began to pray. It didn't move. So we buried our pet with many tears. . . . The kids in our block called me "Prophet Jenkins."[95]

According to Musgrave, play is a very important form of role rehearsal that gives children knowledge of the values and behavior of occupations.[96] In this manner the peer groups in the small southern communities, where games, such as playing church, reportedly are more popular than in the northern cities, have provided informal experimentation with the role of preacher and evangelist.

Religious Background

The deliverance evangelists came predominantly (over 80%) from homes that were at least nominally Protestant. Pentecostal or Holiness sects and denominations formed the largest Protestant subgroup. Others were from Jehovah's witnesses, Quaker, and Mennonite homes as well as from mainline Protestant ones. Seven percent came from Roman Catholic and six percent from Jewish background. In four percent of the families the parents had no religious identification.

Most of the evangelists were exposed during their formative years to ecstatic religious behavior of one type or another. At times the fervor at home was only of transitory duration, and before long the parents backslid to their former "state of sinfulness"; at other times it led to conflicts between the parents, as one parent was "saved" and the other parent, usually the father, rejected salvation vehemently. At least 20 percent of the parents did experience long-lasting religious conversions. The usual trend was from a Baptist, Methodist, or Presbyterian denomination to Pentecostalism.

An illustration of this was the home life of R. G. Hardy, who came from a part-Lithuanian background. Hardy's mother was a devout Roman Catholic but was converted to Pentecostalism through some of their tenants. She began to pray and read the Bible to her children. This infuriated the father so much that he would tear up the Bibles and other religious publications and throw the pieces out the window or burn them.[97]

Another source of observing religious fervor was seeing the dedication of their parents or other relatives as they pursued a religious vocation for which more often than not no great earthly rewards were forthcoming. In approximately one third of the families the father was active in a church-related field. In many other families there was a grandfather, uncle, or some other kin who was engaged in preaching, evangelizing, or simply trying to save souls on his own. In these homes the children could observe the workings of the religious enterprise or they might even be called upon to partake in these endeavors. Thus they gained familiarity with religious role models which they could imitate, identify with, aspire to, and eventually emulate for real in their own career. James Dunn came from one such background:

> My mother and father . . . were not Christian people, although they attended the Primitive Baptist Church. Then Dad and Mom became Christians. They were saved and blessed of the Lord, filled with the precious Holy Ghost and fire, and spoke with other tongues as the Spirit gave them utterance, and Dad was called to preach the gospel. Dad was also doing mining work . . . and went into the coalfields. We moved from mining town to mining town, and Dad would work at the mines during the day and preach at night. He had services in people's homes and in little churches where he pastored. . . . I was raised in a Christian atmosphere in a Christian home. Many evangelists came our way and held revivals for Dad, and I talked with them. . . .[98]

For many their primary source of exposure to the more emotional brand of Christianity was within their own family circle; for others it was their friends, neighbors, or the larger community. The childhood memories to which a number of them look back with nostalgia include playing church with their peers and their mother's prayers for their soul. In many homes the parents not only prayed for them or provided them with religious role models but also wished that they would chose a religious vocation. Especially the mothers were reported to have expressed this desire; but fathers also, if they were in this field themselves, encouraged and aided the attainment of a career in deliverance evangelism.

Oral Roberts' parents had all along hoped that he would become a preacher. When they discovered just before his 16th birthday that Oral was planning to leave home, his mother told him that it had been revealed to them that God wanted him to do something significant with his life. Quentin Edwards explained his interest in religion:

> Dad had prayed to be a missionary. He wanted to go win the boys in the foreign lands, but he never did get to go. He prayed that his children would go, and God has answered his prayers.[99]

Experience with the Healing Arts

The deliverance evangelists seemed to have suffered through the usual childhood diseases, and some of them had been rather sickly during the early years of their life. In this respect they were not too dissimilar from millions of other youngsters across the country. But they apparently often differed in the nature of their interaction with doctors and in their exposure to alternative channels to scientific medicine for the treatment of bodily ills.

In some of the backwoods areas and rural townships no physicians were available. Occasionally disappointing or alienating results occurred from encounters with the medical profession. At times the cost of medical care was beyond the means of their family, and therefore they resorted to various home remedies. Some of these home remedies were crude and painful, such as the one for toothache recalled by W. V. Grant:

> We had no dentist in our community except for one man, across the woods, who used wire pliers; so Papa was our dentist. He had one remedy for the tooth-ache, whether it was caused by a decayed tooth, a cavity, or a tooth broken off. He tied a string around the tooth and "yanked" it out. It worked![100]

The prayers that were offered for their recovery were much more pleasant and soothing, and one became suddenly the center of concerned attention.

Besides being recipients of prayers for God's intervention in their illness process, they were likely to have met people who claimed to have received a miracle of healing or witnessed supposed divine cures taking place. Oral Roberts, for example, saw alleged healings in his father's revivals. In some families medical science was considered inferior to faith healing or was even prohibited altogether.

When Ralph Hart was seriously injured in his youth, his parents fought the authorities to prevent him from being treated by the doctors (see Chapter 5). From these experiences the evangelists learned various techniques of faith healing and something about the psychology of the believers.

Bea Medlin is among those who have testified that prayers for healing were common during their childhood:

> Healing wasn't something new to me because I was taught when a child that healing was for me. When I was very small, I was riding a tricycle which was minus a pedal. As I rounded the corner curb the exposed axle

punctured my left leg. . . : My mother prayed for me and God healed my leg. If I had been hospitalized I probably would have lost that leg. But God spared me that loss and I thank Him for it. I have known the power of God, and it has always been easy for me to believe Him for healing. In fact, healing was more real to me than anything else, perhaps due to seeing my dad and mother ever praying for sick people and seeing them healed.[101]

David Nunn stated:

When I was just a boy, I was converted to Christ in an open-air meeting. As a very small boy, I came in close contact with divine healing, for my pastor at the time was Rev. J. C. Hibbard. He believed in divine healing and had a ministry of healing himself. One day I stepped on a nail which penetrated my foot. I went to Brother Hibbard, and he prayed for me. Instantly all the pain and suffering left! My foot had been healed by the power of God! That was my first experience with divine healing.[102]

Schooling and Work History

On only rare occasions have individuals with a college background ever entered deliverance evangelism. The majority of those evangelists I studied were public school dropouts. Overall, academic achievements were not compatible with their temperament and intersts. They tended to be bored and restless in school, and conflicts with teachers and other pupils were not uncommon. Vic Coburn was permanently suspended from school, others dropped out voluntarily. Dissatisfaction with their days was expressed in many of their life stories.

Leroy Jenkins recalled:

I started to school across the street from my house when I was five years old. School was an unpleasant thing for me. I couldn't get my mind on my studies. There were times when I felt that I could stand it no longer. I would jump up and leave the classroom. I wouldn't go back for the rest of the day. . . . Polly, Harold, and mother started taking turns walking to school with me. They wanted to be sure I got there. There were times when I would run down the long hall and out the opposite end. I would be waiting for mother when she returned home.[103]

M. M. Baker admitted:

When I got to high school I began to grow more interested in rodeo and less interested in my school work. I began to take off from school and go to these rodeos. I missed a lot of school. Therefore, my grades dropped down, down, down.[104]

According to W. V. Grant:

The school children laughed at me for stammering and stuttering. . . . I am so glad that my heart failed me when I intended to kill my teacher. At one time, I had my open knife in my pocket. . . . Another time, I followed the teacher with rocks after he had given me what I considered an unnecessary whipping.[105]

Growing up in the small town of Concordia, Missouri, Kathryn Kuhlman dropped out of high school during her sophomore year and became an evangelist. At one point later on in her career she temporarily gave up the one-night stands on the gospel circuit to pastor a church in Denver. She admitted that for years she had a complex because she had no degrees or seminary training. Of her accomplishments she has remarked, "All I know is what I've learned as I've watched the Holy Spirit work."[106]

Kathryn Kuhlman was among a minority (15%) of my sample for whom evangelism of one kind or another was their very first vocation. The rest had upon leaving school joined the armed forces or plunged into occupations other than evangelism.

Over half of them had previously been ministers or preachers, usually of a small Holiness or Pentecostal congregation. The common patterns here was for certain Pentecostal preachers, such as A. A. Allen and O. L. Jaggers, to be expelled from their position or to resign from it as soon as they felt at least somewhat established regarding finances and compelled to embark on evangelistic ventures.

Close to one third of them had at some time in their lives worked as salesmen or tried to build up a business of their own. Other popular occupations were laborer (primarily factory worker), entertainer (jazz musician, singer, or actor) and occasionally a lower level white collar or clerical worker or some combination of them. Fifteen percent had drifted from one unskilled or temporary job to another. Several of them laid claim to criminal records, often telling stories of their past sins and conversion to Jesus. None of the evangelists had held professional or other high status or influential positions. One of them billed himself as a former M.D., but investigation showed this claim to be false.

Tommy Osborn, son of evangelist T. L. Osborn, confessed that while his parents were overseas saving souls of the heathens, his own was nearly lost for good. When they returned to this country, he had become quite a problem. Tommy gave the following account of the days before he too set out on the gospel circuit:

> The time came when I had pushed Dad too far and I left home. I left with a big row and lots of bad things said that I wouldn't want to repeat. . . . I met Elvis

Presley during this time, and sang with him for a while. I would just go to one place and save enough money to get to the next place. . . . I had been in trouble and out of trouble . . . in jail a couple of times. Dad finally told me, "Son, I just can't afford to have you around running loose. I've got a surprise for you. Get into the car." . . . We drove right downtown . . . right in front of the recruiting office. Before I knew it, I was in the army.[107]

Other Characteristics

Of a review of 71 adult white male evangelists certain similarities were exhibited not only in their mannerisms but also in their physical appearance. Typically they had dark brown or black hair (80%) and at least some tendency towards being overweight (60%). Only 3 percent could be classified as blond and 7 percent as slim or skinny.

Regarding their personality, many of the evangelists were in their youth prone to periods of daydreaming and inner restlessness, according to their life stories. At least 16 percent had run away from home on one or more occasions. Rev. Gordon Lindsay, intimately acquainted both professionally and personally with many of the evangelists, stated that the effective evangelist is usually a high-strung person. He felt that the weakness of some evangelists is emotional instability and that they are more vulnerable to temptations than the average pastor.[108]

The evangelists reported that they have been susceptible to psychic experiences throughout their lives. Besides claiming to have been recipients of miraculous healings, a number of them have also reported having had visions, communications with God and the angels, and/or other apparently paranormal happenings.

Dallas Plemmons stated:

When I was just a little fellow, God would deal with
me. I would go off and sit by myself for hours. Some
of you are going to think that I am an "odd ball." I
didn't completely understand what it was all about, but
I knew that I enjoyed it. We would be in the middle of
a hot ball game. I would just drop the whole thing and
go off by myself. Well, some of the children began to
say I was a "sissy." I resented that with all my heart.[109]

James Dunn related:

It was at Kingston where I had an Angel of the Lord
visit my room. I was about six years old. The angel
sat on the foot of my bed and almost scared me to
death. He sat there for about an hour.[110]

All of them further assert that they were led to enter
deliverance evangelism by a "call from God." By claiming to have received this divine call—and not by any
special training, which is considered unimportant if not
outright harmful—they try to legitimate their assump-
tion of the role of the healing evangelist.

In the life story of "Little Michael" Lord it was reported that he had received his call when he was two
years old and by five had entered his nationwide ministry.[111]

Bud Chambers wrote:

I was only six years old when God spoke to me the
first time. . . . When I was only eight years old, . . .
God spoke to me again. . . . The next time I heard
the voice of God I was 15 years old. I was working in
the harvest fields of westren Oklahoma. . . . I was
working at night driving a big Case tractor . . . when
I heard His voice. He said, 'Preach the gospel to every

creature.' The power of God hit me, I jumped up off
that tractor seat and started preaching right then.[112]

The publications and pulpit pronouncements of the
deliverance evangelists have abounded with narrations
of their own psychic experiences. This may be essential
for building up their ministry. But it also has produced
a loss of credibility in the eyes of the outsiders. In several cases discrepancies have appeared to justify skepticism and rejection of many of these stories. Some of the
more outspoken critics have stated that their claims in
this area prove that they are either frauds or psychotics.
Yet is it not possible that at least some of them have
had certain psychic experiences which they could interpret as a message from the world beyond?

Making the Decision

The gospel circuit has attracted a variety of individuals representing different backgrounds. My investigation
showed that many of them, however, possessed a number of characteristics in common which could be construed as having played an important part in their becoming deliverance evangelists. The findings suggest
that their early upbringing, experiences, prospects for
upward nobility, and type of temperament combined to
bring about their decision.

The parents of a deliverance evangelist were likely to
have impressed on him the doctrine and practices of
some form of the old-time religion and expressed hope
that someday he would become a preacher. If the father
or some other relative held a religious vocation, they
directly provided a meaningful role model along with
possibilities for practical experience and knowledgeable
counseling for his future occupation. Even if the family
was disorganized or of a different religion, the evangelist was often able to observe in his community the per-

formances of Pentecostal pastors and evangelists and the impact they had on his friends and neighbors. Occasionally he himself became the subject of proselytizing efforts. During his leisure time he might imitate the behavior of his elders as he played the game of "church" with his peers. Thus from several directions he was exposed directly or indirectly to influences moving him toward evangelism.

Because of the evangelist's inadequate educational level and disinterest in academic fields, many potential sources of upward mobility were closed to him. He did try other occupations but encountered failure or the rewards were not sufficiently great to continue in them. One of the few legitimate avenues that he might have perceived as open—maybe the only one—for quick upward mobility was deliverance evangelism. He had heard, possibly even witnessed, some of the success stories in this field. He could identify with these individuals, who, after all, seemed not too unlike himself; he had gained valuable experience from his religious background or prior occupations; and he was willing to take a gamble.

Whether his primary motivation was to make money or religious fervor or both—these two need not be incompatible—he also had to be suited psychologically for deliverance evangelism. Possibly the turmoils he experienced in his childhood or some inner restlessness made him receptive to this nomadic occupation. While some of the evangelists do give credit to parental example, encouragement, and training, nearly all of them insist that the crucial factor in their decision was their own psychic experiences—of being saved and receiving a call from God. Supernatural intervention in the career choice remains unverifiable.

Chapter 4

Occupational Subculture

Brother E— was a tall, soft-spoken man. He was in his early 30s and looked more like a football player than an itinerate preacher. The son of a preacher, he had received a call to the ministry when he was in his late teens. His sermons were well presented, and he seemed to have made serious efforts to study the Bible. Regarding the healing of physical ailments, he emphasized that God, not he, heals, and he was willing to pray for the healing of anyone at all, even the most hopeless cases. According to him, faith was important for divine healing, but he admitted that there were cures and failures which he could not explain. I never observed any farfetched narrations nor spectacular miracles at his revivals.

Brother E— was probably a sincere and dedicated man who was greatly concerned with human suffering and sin. There was nothing flippant or patronizing about his behavior. To him deliverance evangelism appeared to be neither a racket nor a means for self-glorification but an important mission that required serious commitment. Yet he was unable to proselytize a sufficient following to continue his calling. He seemed to lack the charisma and the emotional intensity, along with a proficiency for the spectacular to reach the soul and imagination of the people. He journeyed from one town to another, but his fortunes failed to improve, and his earnest prayers went unheralded. Eventually he disappeared from the revival scene. Nothing much is known of him, and his name was readily forgotten by the few who bothered to seek him out. I inquired of several sources as to his whereabouts but nobody appeared to know or care, and the best they could do was to guess that possibly he had quit the gospel circuit.

For every well-known and affluent deliverance evangelist there are scores of obscure and struggling men and women such as Brother E— who travel the hallelujah trail year after year, exhorting the sparse crowd of listeners to believe and have faith. Preaching in tattered tents or dilapidated storefronts, they relate stories of wondrous healings and personal communication with the world beyond. Whether their following is sparse or enormous, they constitute a unique breed of Americans and form an occupational subculture all of their own.

Getting Started:
Success and Failure on the Gospel Circuit

"I received a call from God to enter this ministry," stated Brother E— at one of his revival meetings.

Yet this claim to having received a call from God to bring healing to the sick and save the souls of the sinners was not sufficient to assure his success in deliverance evangelism. He failed. Scores of others who have laid claim to the same divine call have also failed to establish themselves in this ministry. How many unsuccessful attempts there are, no one with whom I talked seemed to know. The names of these evangelists were soon forgotten. Only now and then someone expressed a vague recollection of their fleeting presence.

One of the reasons for failure is that the initiation into deliverance evangelism can be an overwhelming experience, leading to discouragement and consequent withdrawal from it. Noted evangelists, such as Aimee

McPherson, Oral Roberts, A. A. Allen, and Kathryn Kuhlman all reported having spent years of frustrations, insecurities, and struggles to keep their ministry going. Vic Coburn suffered a particularly bitter disappointment when he decided to strike out on his own. Having previously held revivals in churches, he now decided to hold his first city-wide crusade in the small town of Chowchilla, Calif. He admitted having no knowledge of how to plan a crusade nor a proper staff to help him. This did not stop him. He rented the fairgrounds auditorium, printed several thousand handbills, and contacted some local churches and asked for their support. According to Coburn, the crusade was a total loss. The largest crowd only half-filled the place, and the offerings were meager, not even covering his expenses.[113]

Finances can become a crucial survival issue. Evangelists have often had to support themselves through outside sources such as working in a factory or mine. Don Stewart gives a brief accounting of the difficulties those without sufficient connections or financial backing may face: "Holding church along the hallelujah trail was expensive, at least for my budget. I had saved five hundred dollars—enough for only five days of revival at a high school auditorium in my birthplace of Prescott. It would cost one hundred dollars a day for the meeting, forty dollars a night to rent the auditorium, sixty dollars for newspaper ads, radio spots, and miscellaneous expenses. Five days of failure could reduce us to paupers."[114]

According to one estimate it took about a $2,000 investment to buy a tent and start out on the gospel circuit in the 1970s. However, those who aspire to national renown will encounter enormous financial pressures. A moderate ministry that included a monthly publication, about 30 radio stations, and a regular campaign schedule cost in the late 1950s about $3,000 per month.[115]

Thus the neophyte who enters this field with hopes of

quick and easy success may soon find them shattered.
Charles Young admitted:

> I made the same mistake many young preachers make.
> I wanted to be a world famous evangelist and save the
> world overnight. I soon learned you have to crawl
> before you can walk.[116]

Even managing to build up a relatively successful
ministry is no guarantee of continuation in evangelistic
ventures. Oral Roberts, for example, left the field at a
high point in his career. The mental pressures may become unbearable, the life-style may prove tiresome, or
new interests and opportunities may arise. In his comeback try in adulthood, Marjoe Gortner found the financial aspects eventually quite satisfactory. However, after
a while on the gospel circuit other difficulties emerged.
His biography gives the following account of them:

> He was famous. . . . But he was alone. And after a
> while he was forced to admit that the energy flow
> was more and more going one way only: out. The
> responsiveness of his congregations no longer seemed
> to revitalize him, recharge his batteries. Despite his
> greater fluency, his sharpened sense of timing, his to-
> tal professional confidence, it was costing him more
> and more to generate the psychic force that make the
> meetings work. He could do it, but, as the months
> went by, he could do it only as an exercise of will.
> And when a meeting ended, he was empty, flat, worn
> out. . . . The tempo of the life was too strong to
> slacken and ease off, and he wielded his power too
> well to face letting go of it slowly and painfully. In
> the end he supposed it would have to be all or noth-
> ing. But although he knew the end was bound to
> come, he couldn't see it yet. He went on. And it kept
> getting harder, and it started spoiling his taste for
> pleasure, and he went on, and presently nothing was
> any fun—on the road or off it.[117]

Many well-known evangelists have become mentally and physically exhausted from their calling. Rev. Gordon Lindsay observed that only those who have an exceptionally strong physique are able to continue in this type of ministry. The others often settle down and become pastors.[118] After withdrawing from deliverance evangelism, Oral Roberts was able to divert his attention increasingly to such activities as the Oral Roberts University and popular television specials. Marjoe Gortner worked his way into the entertainment field. I was able to conduct a follow-up study of eight more or less small-time evangelists who left a disappointing career. They later ventured into the follow occupations: pastor of a small church, assistant to an established evangelist, gospel singer, manager of a children's home, and temporary odd jobs. They did not, however, necessarily abandon all hope of returning to the revival scene. A few years later at least one of them started to hold revival meetings occasionally in various parts of the country, supporting himself primarily through his pastoral calling.

Then there are deliverance evangelists who continue year after year on the gospel circuit, though they no longer hold visions of fame and riches but only of making just enough to get by. One such evangelist showed up at a small storefront church in Columbus, Ohio, a few years ago. He advertised that many kinds of miracles, including the resurrection of the dead, were taking place during his revivals. But he failed to attract more than a dozen worshipers.

On several evenings I saw him standing in the doorway of the empty church, apparently waiting for anyone at all to show up. Somehow he managed to stay in town a number of months before leaving for another place. He and other obscure evangelists have stayed on for many years in a ministry that brought no earthly riches. Their reasons? Possibly religious fervor, their restless nature, or because "the calling got in the blood," as Marjoe Gortner explained his own stay on the revival scene, though he did not accept its values and beliefs.

Those who eventually are able to achieve at least some amount of success are men and women who can both attract a large following and endure the many demands of their profession. They have to be able to solicit funds and handle administrative problems. Above all they have to possess a charismatic personality in order to assure the growth of their ministry. A number of other characteristics have tended to prevail among them also, which in a variety of degrees have influenced their chances for success and the nature of the occupational subculture.

The socio-economic background of the evangelists was usually quite similar to that of their followers (see Chapters 3 and 6). This helped to sensitize them to the social and psychological needs of potential followers and facilitated communication with these people. They were in a position to have acquired previous insight into the type of people who would be attracted to their brand of religious expression and were able to preach to them what they wanted to hear. The importance of the latter point has been emphasized by Marjoe Gortner. Initially in his comeback try, Marjoe tried to preach what was important to him. He failed with the people. The congregations grew listless, disgruntled, even hostile. Then he changed his preaching to incorporate what he knew these people wanted to hear. His popularity rose immediately.[119]

White, native-born males dominated deliverance evangelism. However, I was assured by many associated with this field—pastors, evangelists, and followers—that no official barriers exist by sex, ethnicity, or race. They maintained that God may call any one of His children, even the most unlikely ones, and bless them with an evangelistic mission.

Women preachers in this country have largely been associated with Pentecostal type of religious groups. In

74

my sample 12 percent (7 out of 60) of the deliverance evangelists were women. Several women deliverance evangelists have been able to attract huge followings and in a couple of cases reached the top position within the profession.

No limits have been set for the age at which an individual may enter deliverance evangelism. I came across reports of a 5-year-old boy and a 100-year-old man traversing the gospel circuit. They, however, have been exceptions. The great majority of the evangelists in my sample were between 25 and 55—an age span during which they are most likely to possess the combination of both the maturity and the stamina essential for this taxing profession.

Many of them were familiar with the Pentecostal community prior to entering evangelism and were able to make the right connection with pastors and others influential in securing backing for preaching engagements. For example, at the church of Rev. Lester Sumrall in South Bend, Ind., I was told that they invite evangelists to hold services there on the basis of recommendation from reliable pastors. The importance of these kinds of opportunities for their careers has been told by numerous evangelists who, particularly if they lacked finances to invest in advertising campaigns and physical facilities, were able to get started and/or continue their ministry by holding revivals at various churches.

Just how desperate the struggle to gain access to a pulpit can get even for seasoned veterans is illustrated by the childhood experiences of Marjoe Gortner. As Marjoe became older and his cuteness faded, his mother's sexual favors allegedly became on occasion one of the fringe benefits for providing bookings for her son. But this was not enough to stay in demand as the charisma was lost. By the time he was 15, both mother and son were working at jobs totally removed from the religious enterprise.[120]

Organizing the Revival Enterprise

The evangelists see some of their colleagues become successful and influential. They see the world take notice of prominent evangelists. They see the conspicuous consumption of Leroy Jenkins and the growing popularity of Vic Coburn. Their own future on the gospel circuit is determined by the number of people they can attract and the amount of money they bring in.

To give people the kind of experiences they expect, and for which they are willing to make financial contributions in return, places strains on the evangelists. According to Rev. Gordon Lindsay, their frantic efforts for a respectable following have led at least some of the healers to use questionable means to attract crowds. Such tactics as fabricating miracles, along with other gimmicks and publicity stunts, and the misrepresentation of the size of the audience by publishing pictures of the crowds of some popular evangelist or "doctoring" the photos to make their own attendance look larger, have been used.[121]

Other quite different methods which have also been used by the evangelists to assure solvency have involved emulating the hard work and entrepreneurship of the business world in the management of the revival enterprise. Though some of the evangelists continue to search haphazardly for speaking engagements, having invested in neither special equipment nor organization, the more career minded have arranged their activities in a systematic manner to maximize efficiency and profits. Typically they have established a nonprofit, tax-exempt organization to carry on their mission. Their headquarters may be found in Los Angeles, Dallas, Delaware, Ohio, or sundry other places. Several have found Tulsa, Okla., a particularly attractive location.

One resident of Tulsa commented that it attracts promoters of fundamentalistic Christian religions of various kinds because "it is old-time Americana, the last of the big cities to offer that."

The range of the evangelists' travels vary, and special efforts may be made to control competition. Marjoe Gortner recalled one such account from his early days on the gospel curcuit. His family's path at one time often crossed those of the Kirkwoods, three brothers well known for their faith-healing ministry. Because of his mother's influence on Brother Andrew, the Kirkwoods agreed not to hit the same towns at the same time.[122]

As the evangelists become more securely established, they turn their activities from simply trying to survive to expanding the variety of their undertakings and sources of income. These ventures may include publishing their own magazine, life story, and other books and pamphlets; marketing gospel records; mailing prayer cloths and other items in return for contributions; providing 24-hour telephone prayer service; having their own radio and television ministry; operating children's homes, Bible schools and nursing homes; sponsoring native churches and oversees aid programs; conducting guided tours to the Holy Land; and holding revivals overseas— some, such as T. L. and Daisy Osborn, spending a substantial part of their time in foreign countries. In addition to personal appearances, the Marjoe Gortner family enterprise, for example, operated in the early days also through record albums, radio, pamphlets, calendars, and a school for infant preachers called "Marjoe's Mission," which actually never even existed[123] but probably was used as a potential for soliciting contributions. According to Marjoe and others familiar with the revival business, several of the above activities, notably the radio ministry, magazine solicitations, and overseas missions, have proven to be financially lucrative for the evangelists. As a more lasting memorial to their ministry a number of deliverance evangelists have eventually established their own church.

The proliferation of activities has given a big business quality to the ministry of such successful evangelists as the late A. A. Allen. Allen rose from poverty to riches not only through his personal charisma but also through apparent organizational ability. He founded his own community, Miracle Valley, Ariz., on 2,400 acres of donated land. In addition to his administrative headquarters, it encompassed a 3,500-seat church, a Bible college, publishing and recording facilities, an airstrip, overnight facilities for guests, and a 250-unit home and trailer subdivision for his employees and others who wanted to live near him and many other activities and programs. At the time of his death he commanded an estimated 400,000 followers, who contributed about $3.5 million annually.[124] Other sources of income included such ventures as selling books and records.

At his death his assistant evangelist, Rev. Don Stewart, took over the enterprise and changed the name from the original "A. A. Allen Enterprises, Inc." to the "Don Stewart Evangelistic Association." Shortly after the takeover, he became entangled in various conflicts, providing the outside world with a glimpse of the difficulties that can beset a complex revival organization.

Stewart was thrown into the difficult position of trying to fill the shoes of someone as charismatic as Allen. Not surprisingly, a decline in popular support occurred. There followed cutbacks in activities at Miracle Valley. The size of the staff was reduced from over 200 to about 65 persons, and the dairy was sold. Stewart and others took pay cuts.[125]

Personality flare-ups surfaced within the organization. Conflicts arose regarding membership on the Board of Directors. One employee was suspected of taking kickbacks as thousands of dollars worth of unused supplies and equipment were discovered. The wife of a top official was fired after she was caught pocketing money from the mail. This incident was followed by the resignation of several persons holding key positions.[126, 127]

The worst was yet to come for Stewart. A lawsuit was filed by ex-Allen officials who wanted to discredit Stewart and remove him from the organization. Among other charges, they contended that Stewart and two bookkeepers had mishandled and embezzled money and that the organization was bankrupt. They obtained a temporary restraining order against Stewart, freezing the organization's assets for six months.[128]

In the end Stewart emerged as the victor. The judge dismissed the suit, stating that the accusers had failed to prove any wrongdoing by Stewart. Later an assistant of the evangelist commented that the lawsuit and resulting rumors had hurt Stewart, but that the organization was back on sound footing. Stewart started to make plans about expanding his radio and television ministry. Mail that was formerly opened by employees is now sent to a Phoenix bank, where the money is removed.[129] Other readjustments and changes followed. A few years after the court case, Stewart was able to report a growth of his overseas ministry and the acquisition of property for a new international headquarters. One of his noteworthy accomplishments has been the expansion and enlargement of the Miracle Valley Bible College, founded by A. A. Allen and now renamed the Southern Arizona Bible College. As of July 1976 all facilities of Miracle Valley were turned over to its use, and a college graduate was appointed as its president.[130]

Don Stewart has not been alone in experiencing intense problems within his organizations. Rather, internal conflict appears almost endemic to independent evangelistic associations. In Vic Coburn's life story allegations were made that it has not been unusual for opportunitists and con men to attach themselves to deliverance evangelists. Often these individuals have moved from one ministry to another. They may be specialists in advertising, skilled copywriters, or experts in the other areas needed in connection with conducting revival meetings. They come to the evangelist proclaiming that they love God and feel they have been sent by God to help him. By performing their tasks diligently, they manage to work themselves up to positions of trust. Once they get the opportunity, they start to line their own pockets through kickbacks, bribes, and theft. On being discovered and asked to leave, they turn to blackmail or extortion. If that does not work they turn to spreading half-truths and false impressions about their former employer. C. A. Roberts credited much of the derogatory information that has been spread about the popular evangelists to disgruntled former associates.[131]

Setting for the Revival Meeting

The deliverance evangelists have held their revival meetings in huge auditoriums, converted theaters, storefronts, regular churches, or "bush arbors." For many none of these places have, however, quite the same atmosphere as the revivals held in a flapping canvas tent.

The tent has become almost a trademark of this ministry, and the acquiring of one's tent has been a primary goal for many aspiring evangelists at the onset of their ministry. There have been problems with tents too. They do not provide protection from the cold, and sounds from them can travel great distances, leading to possible charges of disturbing the peace. Every now and then the tents have been damaged by severe storms. One such incident was reported on the front page of the *Columbus Citizen-Journal*:

Damaging winds and lashing rain hit the Columbus area full force Tuesday night, flattening a revival tent containing 600 persons at the Ohio Exposition Cen-

ter. The congregation escaped serious injury. . . .
The Rev. Wayne Parks Evangelist Crusade tent
crashed down just as the final evening service was
being concluded.[132]

Later on Wayne Parks' journal, *Deliverance Magazine,* carried the following account:

A severe storm warning was out by the U.S. weather
bureau, but we thought the danger was past, so we
went ahead with the service. The beautiful white and
red tent stood like a mountain against the dark sky.
. . . Around 8:00 p.m. our evangelist came to the
platform and spoke briefly. The congregation worshiped God in songs, and the presence of the Holy
Ghost could be felt. Around 8:30 Bro. Parks felt that
the evening service should be concluded at once.
Many could be heard praying as if they all knew
something terrible was about to happen. Hundreds of
people were present when 85 m.p.h. winds came
rushing down the fairgrounds right straight toward
the tent. Wooden poles started breaking in two, the
hooks on the chains were straightened out. The
wooden stakes broke in two like toothpicks. The severe winds pushed the tent over, with many pinned
beneath. Brother Parks was soaking wet by rain, but
many heard him praying out loud, "Oh, Lord, don't
let anyone be hurt." In moments the firemen and policemen were there helping free those under the torn
canvas. Only two people were injured and when our
evangelist prayed for them they were healed. Thank
God!

Someone saw Brother Parks crying as he worked
to free those trapped, saying he had lost all that he
had worked so hard to get for years. . . . Our tent
lay there on the ground, thousands of dollars of lighting and sound equipment looked as if it were ruined.
Our Hammond Organ was knocked over—How
could anything good come out of this?

The next time Brother Parks was seen he was by the side of the blown-down tent praying for the sick and hurt. All of a sudden the Spirit began to move and the amazing Gift that God has given our evangelist was operating. Folks were shouting and speaking in other tongues! The Revival had only begun. The next service night we worshiped God in Christian Center then we moved right back to the fairgrounds and held open-air meetings. By Saturday the tent was back up. The folks of Columbus and surrounding areas had helped us. We thank God that no one was hurt badly, that the folks stood with us in prayers and offerings. . . . After the tent was re-erected, thousands came to worship God. Many healings, miracles took place, and over 1,000 gave their heart to God. One night about 400 were slayed in the spirit as Brother Parks ministered to them, touching none of them. The tent blowing down was a blessing in disguise as we were the leading T.V. and newspaper story. The Lord giveth and the Lord taketh.

The tent has been repaired and we plan to use it again next summer.[133]

Oral Roberts has claimed that the days of the tent are over, that the novelty has worn off, and that the people have become accustomed to soft seats and air conditioning.[134] Though the use of tents has reportedly declined, they have not faded away, and owning the largest tent still is a status symbol. In 1974 Robert W. Schambach claimed that his $50,000 tent was the largest in use.[135] Furthermore, innovations regarding tents have been appearing. One of them was a "pneuma-tent" inflated by a massive compressor.[136]

Tents have continued also for more practical reasons. Marjoe Gortner explained that, after they acquired a tent, they were able to appear at almost any location and could reach more of the rural areas. For evangelists who could attract people in their own right, there have been financial advantages in owning a tent. When the

Gortners appeared at a local church, a division of the offerings, often on a percentage basis, was worked out with the pastor. When revivals were held in their own tent, everything above cost was profit.[137]

Whether the evangelists preach on a raised platform under a tent or on a stage in a theater, the inside setting is usually as austere as the external. Ornamentation and colorful costuming is generally lacking. The more prosperous evangelists have appeared in expensive, stylish clothing. Only occasionally have special kinds of attire or staging been visible. A couple of evangelists have made wearing of sackcloth their trademark. Some have presented special theme nights. Aimee McPherson and O. L. Jaggers and his wife, Velma, have been noted for their spectacular illustrated services. These, however, became a part of their services after they settled down in Los Angeles and no longer had to worry about the problems of carting the special props and equipment from one town to another.

Conducting the Revival Meeting

The revival meetings I have attended over the years have varied considerably, especially in the size of the congregation, degree of emotionality, quality of preaching, and approach to healings. As to similarities they shared, at almost all of the meetings the following traits were present: raising of hands, music and singing, preaching, collecting of money, testimonies, faith healing, exorcism, glossolalia and other forms of trances and saving of souls.

Singing and Preaching Since the days of D. L. Moody an important part of the revival meetings has been the music. Some evangelists sing themselves, others have gospel singers accompanying their crusades. The style of music may be country and western, jazz, or traditional organ performances.

Participation on the part of the congregation is encouraged through singing, shouting "Hallelujah," "Praise the Lord," and "Amen," raising hands heavenward, and giving testimony as to what God has done. For all of these actions Scriptural bases are said to exist.

The evangelists preach in one form or another "that old-time religion," whose essential elements include informality, ecstatic personal experiences, notably speaking in tongues, the literal interpretation of the Bible, emphasis on the role of Jesus and beliefs in miracles, especially in faith healing.

I found many of the sermons repetitious, folksy, and at times quite humorous. They consisted of Bible quotes, critiques of the contemporary scene, personal experiences, and general moralizing. Most of the evangelists also claimed to possess the gift of prophecy, and, either in their sermons or as they picked out some individual while they paced up and down the aisles, they made predictions, usually of a very general nature, of things to come.

To come up with sermons that are vivid, entertaining, and appealing to the congregation is no easy matter. This has been attested to by at least five of the evangelists. One Pentecostal historian maintained that one reason why itinerate evangelism is popular is that the evangelists have a limited number of sermons.[138] Whenever they run out of things to say, it is just about time to move on.

Healings The evangelists have consistently claimed that saving souls is their most important mission—healing is purely secondary. But it is their healing practices which can best pivot them into prominence and wealth.

To establish that they really have a true claim to their ministry, that they actually did receive a divine call to heal the sick, they are expected to demonstrate this gift in public. After all, did not God bless them with it so that they could help the suffering mankind?

Also, according to both their critics and their supporters, making a name for themselves as a healer increases their following. Evangelists Charles F. Parham, Aimee McPherson, F. F. Bosworth, and Marjoe Gortner, among others, have remarked that attendance at their revivals increased significantly after spectacular cures were attributed to their ministry. Vic Coburn stated that 75 percent of his mail comes from nondedicated church people who were initially attracted to his ministry by the healings.[139]

Some variation in the specific techniques of healing do occur. At the revivals I attended, prayers, especially those commanding God to perform a miracle, usually accompanied by the laying on of hands, were the major approach to bring about the claimed cures. Several evangelists stated that they can feel the power of God in their arm when they lay on hands, and they have compared it to electricity. People have also testified to being healed on their way to the prayer line or even while quietly sitting in their seats. In one variation, Smith Wigglesworth practiced, toward the end of his career when he had very large crowds, what he called "wholesale healing" by telling people to lay their own hands on the afflicted part while he prayed for them.[140]

Claims are also made to the efficacy of absent healings, and healings through special prayer cloths and similar items.

A frequent way to organize access to the evangelist for healing purposes is to have a healing line. Generally those who want healing are required to obtain a card at a previously held morning or afternoon service. Many evangelists have found this system to be particularly effective in handling large crowds.

Another method is to call certain categories of people forward. The most common group at the revivals which

I attended consisted of deaf persons. Those suffering from cancer, nervous conditions, and devil possession have also relatively frequently received the invitation.

Many evangelists select individuals from the audience and then pray for their healing. James Dunn, for example, stated that he consistently chooses the people to receive healing one at a time from among those who have congregated to hear his message because God did not want him to have a healing line.[141]

Another evangelist who is opposed to a healing line is Kathryn Kuhlman. When I attended one of her revivals at Notre Dame she stated:

"I am NOT a faith healer. . . . I cannot heal anybody. . . . I don't even know what faith is."

She explained that she was not going to have a healing line nor lay on hands because she did not want to be credited with any cures. According to her, she has nothing to do with the cures nor can she tell how they occur—all she knows is that many people just sitting in their seats are instantaneously made well and rescued from their afflictions. She called only those who had received a healing to come to the platform. And they came in a long procession, one after another, testifying to having received an apparently miraculous, instant cure.

"Do not come up until after you are healed. Do not come to be prayed for," she exhorted.

"There is somebody with a brace. I don't know where you are. . . . I got to go back to the brace."

"There are two sections through here, and a bright bolt of sunshine is coming down," she walked toward the western part of the auditorium. "There is sugar diabetes—at least three healings of sugar diabetes between these two sections. Father, I rebuke the sugar diabetes."

"In the name of Jesus, I rebuke the emphysema. . . ."

Several times during these incidents a person would stand up and affirm that he was the one whose healing she supposedly felt.

At the revival meetings a tremendous variety of illnesses are dealt with. Claims have been made as to the miraculous healing of cancer, VD, TB, paralysis, blindness, deafness, arthritis, broken bones, migraines, tooth cavities, and many other ailments. On occasions the evangelists have engaged in preventive work, such as maintaining that they have just given an instant blood transfusion or prevented an imminent heart attack.

Neal Frisby reported that cures for the following health problems have taken place in his ministry:

> Eardrums, one after another were created; legs were lengthened, one after another. Backbones, nerves, and spinal parts were created. Hip sockets have been created, even when there was no ball. My own brother was born without a knuckle in one hand. I prayed and almost a complete knuckle popped up.[142]

Willard Fuller, specializing in dental evangelism, published the following testimony in his tract "Can God Fill Teeth?"

> Evangelist Fuller conducted a campaign in the church of which I am a pastor. . . . He prays for people and God fills their teeth. I have actually seen fillings appear in teeth that had cavities; some gold, some silver, some white enamel-like substance, and some are completely restored to their original condition.

Even claims to resurrections have been made. James Dunn stated that he had raised one woman from the dead and presented many witnesses to the event. A. A. Allen stated before his death that it is possible to raise the dead but that America is not yet ready for it.

While the surest way to success is to make a name in the area of healing, it is also the most strenuous aspect of evangelism and the cause of much psychological stress and conflict with the larger society. Even one of the most renowned evangelist-healers admitted that his calling is no easy business. To him the healing part was psychologically the most taxing aspect of the profession, with many accompanying stresses and strains. Ineptness at handling the healing line, for example, can destroy one's entire ministry. Furthermore, there can be complications such as lawsuits and investigations by legal and medical authorities. There is also the possibility of getting caught in an embarrassing situation to which there are no easy face-saving responses. If one explains failures too often in terms of lack of faith or failure of God to heal, the people simply will start following one who does produce visible results frequently. A few evangelists have become so insecure at the prospects of attempting to heal that they try to avoid the entire process. I observed a couple of small-time healers who had said that cures of all kinds were taking place at their revivals. Yet night after night they kept the meeting going till the audience became exhausted and commenced to leave, and so they just never did get around to saying so much as a prayer for the sick.

Exorcism and Other Miracles Many evangelists have emphasized that God does not send disease and that disasters are not an act of God. Rather, these and other misfortunes that beset mankind are said to be caused by evil spirits. Adolf Hitler and Joseph Stalin have been used as examples of Satan in human form. Thus an integral part of the work of the evangelists consists of exorcism—the driving out of the devil from supposedly possessed victims. Oral Roberts stated that he could recognize devil possession.

> First . . . I feel God's presence, usually through my hand; then I catch the breath of a person—it will have a stench as of a body that has been decayed; then I notice the eyes. They're like snake eyes.[143]

The actual driving out of the devil consisted usually of loud exhortations to God and the laying on of hands.

Other forms of thaumaturgy are now and then also presented at the revivals as the congregation is urged to believe for a miracle. Gordon Lindsay stated that evangelism should be accompanied by a ministry of the supernatural, for Jesus supposedly defined this type of work as one to be followed by miraculous signs in Mark 16:15-18. Yet Lindsay has also been quite unimpressed by some of the claims of supernatural, stating that sensational publicity stunts are no substitute for the Gospel. He criticized a case where the minister tore the shirt off his back and declared that it had some unusual virtue calling for a special offering. In another case the preacher suddenly shouted that he saw an angel walk upon some tent shavings, which were gathered into a wash tub and mailed out in small quantities to people giving offerings.[144]

Yet many similar events keep on occurring, such as:

Aimee McPherson in Arkansas City, Kans., bade the rain clouds disperse, and her followers testified that they obeyed. At least two other evangelists have been credited with rain control ability.

According to Leroy Jenkins, God told him that He was giving him a special sign so that people would know he had a miracle arm. This sign was that Leroy's thumb and next two fingers, representing the Father, Son, and Holy Ghost, on his right hand would turn red as if covered with blood, and he stated that this has occurred at several of his revivals.[145]

At an A. A. Allen Miracle Revival, God supposedly poured supernatural oil out of seven-year-old evangelist Lewin Burchan's hands. Along with anointing the little boy with miracle oil, it was claimed that God instructed him to lay his oily hands upon the sick for healing. Following this incident, many in Allen's meetings reportedly rushed to the platform, their hands dripping also with supernatural oil. According to Allen, from that time this phenomena has spread to other parts of the world. He explained this apparent miracle by Ps. 45:7: "Thou lovest righteousness and hatest wickedness; therefore God, thy God, hath anointed thee with the oil of gladness above thy fellows."[146]

Several evangelists have claimed to have visited heaven and have written tracts of this experience, giving detailed descriptions of what they supposedly saw there. One evangelist was reported to have spent many revival meetings discussing his trip to heaven. Yet when his autobiography came out a few years later there was not a word of this extraordinary experience, though there were many descriptions of travels on this earth.

Collecting Money To carry on their work the evangelists obviously must have financial support. They have many huge expenses that are not readily apparent to those attending their revivals. Freewill offerings make up a substantial, to a number of them the only, source of income.

Methods of collecting money vary considerably. At many revivals I attended, the collection of money was handled very discreetly and in low key. At others, extensive high pressure tactics and gimmicks of all sorts were used.

At least two evangelists have used what they called the Holy Ghost Clothes Line. On one such occasion a rope was stretched around the auditorium with clothes pins hanging from it to which people were to attach their donations and, according to one evangelist, if enough money was put on it the Holy Ghost Himself might come down. On one occasion quite a few bills and pledges were hung on it, but the Holy Ghost did not materialize. However, the evangelist did maintain that He was near and that he could feel His presence, to which most of the audience replied "Amen."

At a large tent meeting one evangelist asked people to contribute $100 and guaranteed that God would pay them back, adding casually, "And even if God doesn't give it back to you, what's a hundred dollars?"

Many deliverance evangelists have stated implicitly that the more one gives the more likely one will receive health, happiness, and especially wealth. Testimonies, particularly in the publications of the evangelists, from happy contributors abound.

"You can't outgive God," is a frequent expression heard at the revivals.

Psychic Experiences: Trance and Being Saved After the money has been collected, the sermon preached, and the sick dealt with, the evangelists usually call all those who want to be saved to come forward. It is during this stage that I have witnessed some of the more extreme manifestations of dissociation states. However, the dissociation states or trances can occur at any time during the revival and may take diverse forms, such as: the jerks, ranging from mild trembling in upraised hands to violent convulsions, involving such behavior as the snapping of the neck and whiplike movements of the spine; rapid dance-like movements; falling to the floor, either with jerks or remaining still as in a faint; running in a straight line up and down the aisles; and glossolalia, or speaking in tongues.

Scientists have hypothesized that trance may represent hypnosis, non-pathological dissociation, socio-cultural learning, histrionics, and epilepsy.[147] To the believers this form of behavior, particularly speaking in tongues, has deep religious significance. A number of persons have told of being healed of both physical ailments and psychological problems after speaking in tongues. A sense of joy and a deep religious emotion has often been reported as accompanying it.[148] According to Don Stewart:

. . . all believers are commanded to be filled with the Holy Spirit, and . . . the initial physical evi-

dence of this infilling is the same as that received by
the believers at Pentecost: speaking in tongues. . . .
This experience should be the beginning of a life of
ever-increasing power for testimony and service.[149]

The evangelists and their aides exhort the believers to
obtain these trance states. They have made statements
to the effect that the more extreme the trance the
greater the religious fervor, that these states are God's
means of communicating and that the state of the believer's soul is indicated by physical symptoms, such as
speaking in tongues.

At the revivals I attended, I observed that women
were more likely to go into a trance than men and
blacks more likely than whites. Also the extent and nature of the trance state has varied from the revivals of
one evangelist to another.

At the conclusion of one revival meeting I attended
at the Full Gospel Tabernacle, the evangelist asked all
those who wanted to be saved to come forward. Over
30 souls responded to his call, while most of those who
had remained in their seats began to head for the exit.
The evangelist recited a short prayer for those kneeling
before him and quickly left. Several of his assistants remained, going from one individual to another and urging them to repent. Many went into a trance. One
woman began to swing blindly in all directions; another
executed a "spirit-filled" dance with rapid, jerky movements. Seven girls, ranging approximately from age five
to ten, fell into a deep dissociation state, calling out
for Jesus. A woman had them kneel down and lean on
the edge of the stage and kept a careful eye on them. Two
young Negro men went into an especially agitated
trance with one of them acting similar to someone having an epileptic seizure. The moanings, mutterings, out-
cries, and prayers were to a large extent drowned out by
rapid drumbeats. It was not until the musicians began to
depart that the participants began to come out of their

trances, some easily, others being comforted and talked to by their companions. A short time later, when the lights were dimmed, only a few souls remained.

A young woman sat in the front row, quietly sobbing, "Jesus, forgive me. Please, forgive me. Oh, Jesus!"

A man in overalls sat patiently near his wife, who was lying prostrate on the floor. Gently he had placed a worn army blanket around her.

"Esther, its time to go home," he whispered.

The woman barely stirred.

And so another revival meeting came to an end.

Chapter 5

The Faith Healer, His Family, and the Greater Society

The deliverance evangelists may find themselves in a marginal position—criticized, looked down upon, and, at times, drawn into bitter conflicts with their fellowmen. They also have to make adjustments to the insecurities, stresses, and rootlessness of the gospel circuit. All this has an impact on their relations with the greater society and on the nature of their family life.

Occupation Versus the Family

Being Married to an Evangelist The great majority in the sample of evangelists I studied were married. Most of them had one or more children. Their own families were, on the average, smaller than those of their parents. Their comments on the subject consistently espoused a stable, close-knit, traditional style of marriage and family life. At revival meetings I repeatedly heard pronouncements against immoral behavior, divorce, and neglect of families.

Not all the evangelists were able to realize these ideals in their own private lives. There were cases of separation and divorce involving, for example, Aimee McPherson and Leroy Jenkins. But their careers apparently did not suffer on account of it. Neither did Kathryn Kuhlman's divorce hamper her eventual success as an evangelist, though it did create problems for her at the time. It all occurred back in the late 1930s while she was the head of a large congregation in Denver. One of the guest speakers at her church was evangelist Burroughs A. Waltrip, who decided that he liked Kuhlman better than his own wife. After his divorce became final, he married Kuhlman in Mason City, Iowa. This marriage, however, did not last long, and the ensuing scandal ended Kuhlman's career in Denver.[150]

"Divorce is something our religion is opposed to," one evangelist's wife, who had been married for more than 30 years, told me. She admitted that being married to an evangelist can place strains on the relationship. His frequent absence from home can be particularly hard to handle—something she herself had lived through but preferred not to voice complaints about.

Couples with close, long-lasting marriages have also experienced disagreements and fights over occupational demands and commitments. One of the critical points in the lives of several of the couples occurred when after marriage one of the spouses made the decision to become a deliverance evangelist. This action was to entail sudden, radical changes in the life-style of the entire family, which not all of them felt able or willing to cope with.

Reportedly the decision of one man to become an evangelist led to such heated fights with his wife that the police had to intervene. Only much later did she resign herself to the situation and become reconciled with her husband.

Lorene, the darkhaired, active wife of Rev. W. V. Grant, tells that she was far from pleased when she found out about his decision:

In our house, one day I found several pages my husband wrote to me. He acknowledged that he was called to preach. He said he was going to sell our businesses. After crying awhile, I told him I would stay at home and make him a living and let him go and preach. I was not willing to sell the home or the business, but I would rent them. He was not willing to do that. He listed everything for sale. It was hard for me to say "yes," but I did.[151]

Once established in the occupations, the evangelists and their families must continue to make accomodations to changes in the ministry or the family. The financial ups and downs of this calling, legal problems, the birth of a child, illness, education for children, and other life crises all need special adjustments.

Kathy, the wife of Rev. Don Stewart, is one of the numerous spouses who has had to work hard and make personal sacrifices to minimize the disruptive aspects of the occupational subculture on family stability. She is a very attractive blond woman who greatly resembles a youthful Grace Kelly. At the time I first met her, her husband had more than a year ago taken A. A. Allen's place. This transition in particular had been quite difficult for her, as with the unexpected death of Allen both of them were suddenly shouldered with all kinds of new responsibilities and pressures.

Unlike the families of evangelists who participate actively as a team in all aspects of conducting revivals and sometimes even compete with one another, Kathy has only occasionally sung at the services or otherwise appeared in the limelight. One example of some of the activities in which she has partaken is her photo report of her husband's London crusade in the December 1975 issue of *Miracle*.

I found Kathy a charming person, cordial and relaxing to talk to as we discussed the good and the bad times on the gospel circuit and her feelings about it.

I am basically a shy person. I don't like to be the center of attraction. I prefer to stay in the background, to be an observer rather than a participant. As for running the campaign, I'm just not interested in the problems and business aspects.

From the many years of having been part of the revival world, Kathy has become cognizant of the strains connected with it and how they can affect individuals, tear into even the closest relationships and why therefore it was necessary for one of them to be outside the field as much as possible.

I want to avoid the pressures that are part of Don's work so that when he comes home I can provide him with an environment in which he can relax. I want to be free when he is free so that we can be together and do things jointly.

Other wives also, particularly if they have found personal fulfillment and recognition in supplementary roles, have supported the work. They may perform onstage in the services, help with the collection of money, edit publications, mail out requests for contributions, and in sundry ways perform essential tasks.

"After marriage my main function has been that of a helpmate," stated Louise, the wife of Rev. Lester Sumrall, as she described her role to me. They first met in Argentina where she was a Canadian Assemblies of God missionary and he a deliverance evangelist holding overseas crusades. Her own involvement has included preaching, personal witnessing, working with youth and women's groups, and typing manuscripts.

Occasionally a wife has taken over the ministry after her husband's death and has established a reputation in her own right. Daisy Osborn, who for 25 years had ministered across the world with her husband, T. L. Osborn, has started to set out in solo missions—the first one to a Nigerian monarch.[152]

But not all wives have been so supportive or enthusiastic over their husband's calling. One wife reportedly threatened to have her husband committed to a mental hospital if he did not quit the gospel circuit. Lexie, the wife of A. A. Allen, also allegedly filed insanity proceedings against him twice. In his divorce suit against her, charging her with cruelty, Allen requested that she be prevented from trying again to commit him.[153] Another wife stated that she has placed various pressures on her husband to leave the gospel circuit:

> I'm not the only one against it. . . . All I want is for him to leave. . . . There are many opportunists hanging around him, trying to influence him, coming between us. . . . It would be better all around if he just quit.

The Strains of Separation The most frequently mentioned sources of conflict between their family life and occupation were the separations from spouse and children, continued traveling, education of children, and dealing with the expectations of other people.

Some wives, particularly those with young children, stayed away from the gospel circuit and remained at home. While this has sheltered them from many of the strains, it has led to others. They have complained of loneliness, of the growing estrangement between them and their spouse, and of mutual suspicions, real or imaginary, regarding the others fidelity.

Kathy would have liked being a full-time housewife settled in her own home. While she felt that there was much that was positive in the less radical aspects of the women's movement, she herself wanted to try to be as good a wife and mother as possible. Her major concern was that her entire family should stay together. For while they were together now, it was not always that way.

Previously, when the children had to attend school, Don had been able to get home maybe only twice a month. The two or three days he was at home he was generally busy with the many details of his work.

> I was very lonely. It was also a difficult period for Don. He used to call long distance all the time. But talking to the children over the phone is not the same as being at home. I firmly believe that a boy needs a father who is at home and with whom he can converse in person.

She busied herself with taking care of the home, sewing, and art classes from a nearby junior college—activities that she enjoyed greatly but that could not take the place of an absent husband.

On the Road Possibly because of her zeal or previous religious activities, Louise did not mind the traveling and stated that she experienced no particularly serious problems. The greatest difficulty that they faced was in communicating with people in certain non-Western areas where very few knew English.

Many others have felt quite differently about being on the road. Next to being separated from her husband, by far the most difficult thing for Kathy has been the constant traveling. They have a lovely home in Arizona but have spent comparatively little time there.

Living in a trailer, she had the problem of keeping her two active children entertained and still have some peace and privacy for herself.

> "It was especially difficult when the children were smaller. There were problems of finding laundry facilities, and so many other difficulties emerged which people settled in their homes would not face. . . . Previously we had to search for baby-sitters. But now we have a girl to take care of the children, and it works out much better."

Kathy admitted that she has resigned herself to this nomadic existence at least for the time being:

"Other people live like this too. I am not the only one to have problems."

There have been other shortcomings too for the Stewart family. All of them are tired of eating out. The trailer does not provide sufficient space to develop their hobbies. Kathy has been concerned about finding proper peer groups for her children. And it has been exhausting.

Frequent complaints of the evangelists and their wives were that they are tired of being constantly on the move, living in motels, and eating at hamburger joints. A couple of the wives felt that this life-style, with its nervous pace, might have been responsible for the weight problem of their husbands and posed difficulty for staying on a strict diet.

Several wives said that they suffered from boredom. Kathy, however, stated that this was not a problem for her. She spent her free time going to museums, the zoo, on walks, or socializing with various members of the crew. But she did miss having close friends around her to whom she could confide personal concerns and worries.

Lorene also spent much of her time accompanying her husband at the onset of his career. Being at that time in more austere circumstances than the Stewarts, she recalls the travails of the life on the road when they were still struggling to establish themselves:

My husband had a drive that pushed him on. He would be in such a hurry to go to the next revival that I've seen him actually blow the car horn for a red light to change. We would drive up to 800 miles in a day. We'd travel without air conditioning all afternoon, facing the sun. . . .

101

We stored our prized possessions under my mother-in-law's house. The rats got into the boxes and ate the things up. . . .

One time we stopped at a hotel about 11 p.m. It turned out to be a bad house. The girls had customers all night. To get away from the place, we hit the road the next morning at 4 a.m. It was a bitter cold morning. We ran out of gasoline before daybreak, miles from nowhere. Junior and I lay down in the seat to keep people from seeing us while Brother Grant walked down the cold road hunting for gasoline. . . .

It was our policy to never leave a revival regardless of what came against us. In one home, the preacher's wife nagged at him nearly all night in the next room. We almost broke that rule. We were about to pack up and be gone before daylight. She would go into an angry fit at the table, then run and fall on her face like a child. The pastor explained that these attacks came on each month. Brother Grant said, "I think each attack lasts thirty days". . . .

Brother Grant was determined to let nothing stop him. One time he broke his zipper. He just put a handkerchief over his belt and prayed people through until about midnight. . . .

In one revival, we stayed in a little house where the lady washed dishes only once a week. We took a bath in a washtub. We had to wade water to get to the outdoor restroom. The church paid them for keeping us, but we went to the store and bought our own groceries. The man and woman slept in the front room. They would fuss because we woke them up after church. About the time we went to sleep one night, the bed fell with us. We propped it up with a water jug. The next day we had to pay for the bed and the jug.[154]

Education of Children The problems of traveling become particularly accentuated in families with young children, the schooling of the children becoming a vital concern.

One evangelist stated that his children had to change schools every few weeks. There were further difficulties as they went through the usual childhood illnesses—though God did heal them, these things nevertheless were disruptive. He decided then that for the children to receive proper schooling his family had to stay behind at some central point in relation to his circuit. Both he and his wife said that they found this separation quite difficult but necessary.

Lorene also found that it was difficult to provide for children:

> While driving down the road one day, our 10-year-old boy burst out crying. He couldn't quit. He said, 'I wish I could have a home like other boys.' I cried a little too. In one home they told him to play with the toys. In another home, they told him not to bother the toys. He didn't know what to do.

> When he was in the fourth grade, he had been to 42 states and 42 schools. He learned his letters by reading the signs. "EAT." He learned his figures by watching the speedometer on the car, wanting to know when he could eat.[155]

Kathy was at least for the time being more fortunate, for she and Don felt they were in a position now to provide private tutoring.

"I plan to hire a teacher to travel with us. A couple of the members of our team also have children, and they too would like to have their families accompany them."

Depending on the finances and the eventual future goals of the children, the kind of education the Stewarts were planning for their offspring might provide some very definite advantages. Marjoe Gortner was reported to have stated that his early years were not misspent, despite the fact that he had an abnormal childhood:

> My parents had me tutored so I never went to a regular school. But from age 4 to 15 I had the best acting training in the world, preaching every Sunday and almost ever other night of the week.

> I was surrounded by adults all the time. I watched and studied people and learned.

> Look at it this way . . . I traveled in every state of the Union and by the time I was 9 I had toured Europe. That was a real education. I think it outweighs the fact that I was exploited and worked as a child.[156]

Not all of the evangelists have been able to afford private tutors. Others have felt that it would be cumbersome to have the children along or that the children might be better off attending regular school and being with others their own age. Kathy also worried how their life-style was going to affect the education and social adjustment of the children. She hoped that they would grow up to be good Christians in the Pentecostal tradition, but she would not push them into a religious vocation nor try to convince the boy to follow in his father's footsteps.

"I want them to make up their own minds."

The children of the evangelists were on the average getting more formal education than their parents, and it was generally expected that they would complete high school. Vocationally some of the offspring have done reasonably well in related endeavors. But overall it is highly unlikely for a second generation of successful evangelists to emerge. So much depends here on personal charisma, which cannot be passed on from parent to child.

Meeting the Expectations of Others Like scores of other wives Kathy has fluctuated between staying behind at home and being with her husband. She clearly prefers the latter but feels the disadvantages of the pressures of the work.

At times she has been swarmed by the followers of her husband and has been somewhat at a loss for knowing what to do:

"Many bring their problems to me. Sometimes they even come in the middle of the night and pound on the trailer door. Their sad stories can be very depressing, but I try not to let them get me down."

One of the problems she has faced repeatedly is one that is quite familiar to the spouses of clergymen. Like her husband, she and the children are pressured to conform to a particular mold and subjected to different expectations than other people.

Being an evangelist's wife, people expect you to conform to a certain image. They expect you to react and act in a certain way. But I want to be me. I want people to accept me for what I am. . . I am not an outgoing person. I am not aggressive. And I don't want to change. . . . Also many people feel that behavior that is quite acceptable to them is not acceptable for me. They expect me not to do what they do."

Several wives of clergymen have observed that people have not been open with them because of their position. Kathy has experienced this also:

I can sense that people don't always feel at ease in my presence. . . . Often there appears a barrier between me and them—like I am not supposed to be like others. People hesitate with me. I have to continually reach out—then they respond. But I have to take the first step. Even friends avoid talking about certain things in my presence.

To some extent this also extends to her children. They also have at times received differential treatment because they are "preacher's kids."

> Some people tell them "How could you do that, being a preacher's son?" I don't think it's fair to expect different behavior from them than from other kids. Then there are people who go to the other extreme and shower them with attention and favors, really pampering them. This also isn't good.

Occupation Versus the Greater Society

The Prosperity Gospel   One area where in particular the expectations of others and the life-style of the evangelists and their families have clashed has been the apparent material prosperity and conspicious consumption that many of the evangelists enjoy.

I have attended the revivals of evangelists who might quite possibly be leading, voluntarily or involuntarily, an austere existence. Their congregations were small. Their sermons contained no promises of earthly riches to those who adhere to God's commandments. Their clothes were inexpensive and had seen much wear over the years. Other signs of affluence were also missing. But these evangelists have been overshadowed by their more successful colleagues, whose display of wealth has received widespread notice.

One such evangelist is Leroy Jenkins. He lives in a mansion filled with glitter and ornate objects, many of them gifts from his followers. Of the overabundance of ornateness he stated:

> I like that. I'm Indian. . . . I like real loud and real nice things 'cause I never had them. . . . Most people in my crusade have made commitments . . . chandeliers, Cadillacs.[157]

106

Kathryn Kuhlman, according to a UPI report, allegedly had under her home a walk-in vault for her money and collected over $2 million worth of art and jewelry.[158]

Many Americans have viewed these life-styles of the evangelists with misgivings. One man stated:

> Somehow it doesn't look right if a man of God is interested in material things. It goes against the principles of early Christianity. . . . He should lead a spiritual and simple life. Otherwise, his motives and sincerity are suspect.

Others have expressed similar ideas.

The following incident occurred to W. V. Grant as told by his wife Lorene:

> We traded for a secondhand Cadillac. We stored it in Seattle during the meeting. We received a letter from a lady in Seattle while we were in Los Angeles. It said 'I almost had a man converted; when he learned you had a Cadillac, I lost him.' We traded the car off for the sake of the work of God. We got a more expensive car, but one with another brand name.[159]

One evangelist told me that he has always liked big, expensive cars. He saw nothing wrong in it. Furthermore, being constantly on the road these cars are more practical and comfortable. Yet he has been criticized by both followers and outsiders for owning them. He stated that he really resented that in this and other areas he had to modify his life-style to what he felt were unrealistic demands.

He and the other evangelists have grown up in this society which emphasized materialistic values. They have internalized these values. They like mod clothes, fancy cars, and material comfort just like many other

Americans. Because they come from a lower socio-economic background, their taste may well tend to gravitate towards flashiness. Now they discover that as men of God they are expected not to enjoy these earthly pleasures but are to be ascetic.

Overwhelmingly they have come to reject an austere existence. They have explained that "God's people deserve the best." Oral Roberts, who has been extensively attacked for his affluence, was quoted to have said that he was not going to apologize for buying the best:

"God doesn't run a breadline. The idea that religious people have to be poor is nonsense."[160]

David Nunn explained:

Some time ago God spoke to my heart about prosperity for his people. One of the great hindrances to faith for finances is the doctrine of poverty. . . . this poverty doctrine has enslaved God's dear children with the idea that it is blessed to be poor. The Scriptures declare that 'Blessed are the poor in spirit.' This has nothing to do with finances, for to be poor in your pocketbook is neither blessed nor convenient.[161]

The evangelists in general have been promoting a prosperity doctrine of one kind or another. They have indicated that God not only wants men to be healthy but also wealthy, and their followers have been encouraged to work for and enjoy such unspiritual things as automobiles and color television sets. Scores of them have preached sermons and written articles and books claiming that to prosper financially it is necessary to donate money generously to God's work. One evangelist, for example, delineated three steps to riches: First, do what is right in God's sight. Then work enthusiastically, since money is not going to come by accident. Finally, have faith and risk something—such as a substantial contribution for a "prove me" offering to the evangelist.

Scientific Medicine Though many of the evangelists have come to accept what the world has to offer in terms of material goods and comforts, there are many other areas of secular life towards which they have come to express ambivalent feelings or even outright rejection. One such area is scientific medicine.

Finding themselves in competition with the physicians, the deliverance evangelists have traditionally tended to reject medical science. One of the pioneers of this profession, Mary B. Woodworth Etter, wrote in her book *Questions and Answers to Divine Healing:*

> The greater portion of the physicians of the land are ungodly people, many of them professed infidels, and never were designed of God to administer drugs and poisons to anyone; much less the people of God whose bodies are the sacred temples of the Holy Spirit.[162]

Today most of them no longer denounce medicine as the work of the devil; the physicians' diagnosis and prognosis seem to be rather well accepted and a few evangelists have even shown a relatively tolerant attitude toward it.

The public stance taken by the evangelists may be summarized as one of condescendence and superiority towards scientific medicine. Undercurrents of hostility can be felt often through innuendos, criticisms, and advice that is contrary to that of the sufferer's physician. The emotional, spectacular, and instantaneous nature of the cures proclaimed at the revivals overshadow anything done in the medical setting. Though considerable variation exists in attitudes, nevertheless, it can hardly be said that this healing ministry promotes confidence in the use of scientific medicine.

Some of them view medicine as only marginally helpful. More often than not, they maintain, it is ineffective—many patients who have been given up by doctors have received healing at the revival meetings. They have repeatedly emphasized that scientific medicine is at most second best.

Kathryn Kuhlman affirmed that she is not against doctors. Had she chosen a profession, it would have been medicine or law. But in this she had no choice, since God called her to preach the Gospel. According to her, God does work through medicine, since all healing, physical and spiritual is divine. But of the two, the spiritual is by far the superior.[163]

Gordon Lindsay wrote:

I thank the Lord for physician friends, but I must testify that as God has revealed Himself as my Great Physician, I have always felt that I must lean upon Him alone.[164]

Furthermore, Lindsay felt that in many instances going to a doctor would hinder one's faith:

Physicians serve a valuable purpose and, of course, we are not opposed to them. Doctors are able to give valuable advice as to the care of the body, proper diet, etc. The Bible teaches that we should obey the laws of health. There are instances, however, when God is specifically dealing with an individual to get him to put his trust in Him. Relying on medical drugs might in that case weaken his faith.[165]

Holding the more extreme position on medicine, one evangelist argued that many times physicians, who have been placed on earth for those who do not trust the Lord, actually make the patient's condition worse. The central question, according to him, was "Why don't you trust the Lord?"

A few have openly stated that they themselves would under no circumstance make use of any physicians.

"Only God Heals" has been the motto of several evangelists.

The doctrine espoused regarding medical science can have an impact not only on the practices of the followers but also on those of the faith healers themselves and their families. Faith healers who attack medical science and who maintain that only God heals but, nevertheless, would like to seek secular treatment for their own ills may find themselves in an awkward position and threatened with a loss of credibility.

In one case the evangelist had gone to considerable efforts to hide the fact that he had been hospitalized. Another evangelist, A. A. Allen, stated that God does not heal through medicine and that those who trust God have no need of secular physicians. He went on to present scary details of what physicians do to patients, contrasting it with the ecstacy of God's healing.[166] Yet he himself had entered a hospital shortly before his death, and when his body was discovered, police found several vials of pills in his possession.[167]

Overall I found that at least a number of evangelists have used the services of secular physicians. Quite possibly, however, they try to minimize and delay contact with the medical professions. C. A. Roberts reports of a successful faith healer of the 1960s who for three weeks endured his illness without seeking outside aid. Finally when he was taken to a hospital, the doctors stated, according to Roberts, that they could have helped if they had gotten to him sooner.[168]

Some faith healers appear to believe totally in divine cures and unquestioningly try to follow their own teachings. I have read about faith healers who to the very end refused any outside treatments. Others, under less spectacular conditions, have also tried to rely only on God for the cure of their ailments. Sometimes when it has involved other members of their family, conflict with the greater society has ensued. One such case was that of Ralph Hart; it received considerable publicity in the mass media.

The Story of Ralph Hart

On a Monday night around 10:00 o'clock, while working after school as a Western Union messenger, 16-year-old Ralph Hart was hit by a drunken driver, who did not even bother to stop his automobile. An ambulance took Hart to a hospital, where he was found to be suffering from a broken collar bone, possible skull fracture, and bleeding from the ears. He was given standard emergency treatment immediately. His condition was listed as grave, and chances for recovery were felt to depend largely on an immediate operation.

His parents did not receive the notification of his accident till about 1 a.m., when the police found them as they left their church after a prayer meeting. The parents were stunned by the news and rushed immediately to the bedside of their unconscious son.

The doctors wanted to operate, feeling that it was essential for the boy's recovery. But the father, a full-gospel evangelist, was adamantly opposed to the idea.

"God is our hope. He will take care of my boy," agreed the mother.

She did permit his head to be bandaged, but an operation was out of the question as far as she was concerned.

Later, when the doctor once more pressed the father to sign the papers permitting the operation, Rev. Hart stated:

"Sir, you'll do nothing of the kind. He's in God's care now. When he was just eight years old, he fell off our barn across a tree stump and broke his back. God took care of that without your help, and He's gonna take care of this, too."[169]

The father later complained that he was blocked

The upraised hands of Kathryn Kuhlman.

John Alexander Dowie.

G. O. Barnes.

Ralph Hart, stricken son of the Rev. and Mrs. L. M. Hart, after his parents permitted science to aid prayer in his recovery.

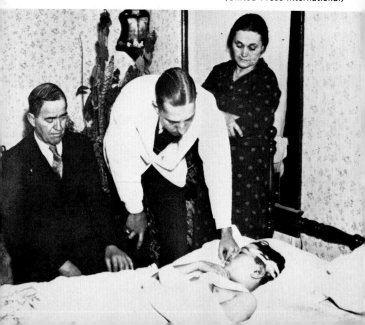

On the broad platform of her Angelus Temple in Los
Angeles, Sister Aimee Semple McPherson leads the
singing in her regular Sunday night service.

(Wide World Photos)

Hands raised en masse during a prayer meeting conducted by Kathryn Kuhlman.

Kathryn Kuhlman
leading a service.

Kathryn Kuhlman touching the cheek of a woman seeking her help at a rally in Detroit.

Reverend A. A. Allen.

Jack Coe in the courtroom, Miami, Fla. The Texas Evangelist was accused of practicing medicine without a license.

Oral Roberts.
(Oral Roberts University)

Oral Roberts, at work.

(Oral Roberts University)

Oral Roberts during the ritual of 'laying on of hands.' *(Oral Roberts University)*

Leroy Jenkins' opulent quarters.

(George DeVault)

Marjoe Gortner, at the age of five, preaching to an audience of 1,200 in Long Beach, California.

(Wide World Photos)

Marjoe!

Little Michael praying for the sick.

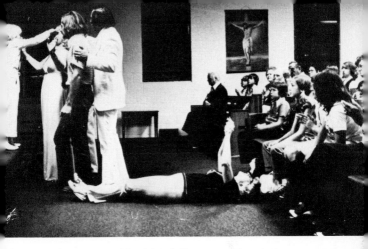

Little Michael with his followers who have come forward to be healed.

(Wide World Photos)

Mourners gathered at the funeral of the Reverend William Branham.

(Wide World Photos)

Reverend Don Stewart.
(Wide World Photos)

Roxanne Brandt.
(Roxanne Brandt Crusades)

W. V. Grant.
(W. V. Grant)

Lorene Grant,
wife of W. V. Grant.
(W. V. Grant)

CAN GOD FILL TEETH

Thousands claim this miracle
in the ministry of
Evangelist Willard Fuller
A Man of God
for These Special Day

The Love of God, The Joy of the Lord
The Gifts of the Spirit Flow through
these vessels to the Glory of God.

ELIOT-WILLARD FULLER
P.O. BOX 975
MOUNTAIN VIEW, CALIF. 94

A Miracle Ministry
The Holy Spiri

The deeper truths of God preached from the Bible to me
der's world.

A Ministry for the New Age:
Teaching, healing, helping to move on into the gr
het for His children.

Let us go on unto perfection, to words peace and
each individual. Let the things that keep us fro
Everything be healed.

The prayer a
Our God is a

We
P.O.

THE MIRACLE MINISTRY OF
WAYNE PARKS

Coming to Columbus, Ohio

OLD FASHION
REVIVAL
EVERYONE COME AND HEAR

NORMA JEAN
ATWOOD

Sing the Gospel Under the
Anointing of God

Preach the Gospel in the
Old-Time Way

REVIVAL TIME IS HERE
The Full Gospel Preached And Received
According To: John 14:14

REVIVAL

Monday, July 24th - First Service 7:45 p.m.

Evangelist Rex Gwaltne

OF CHEYENNE, WYOMING

WITH

Song Leader – Norma Jean Atwood
Organist and Pianist – Carol Lewis

GOD HAS GIVEN THIS YOUNG MAN AN UNUSUAL MINISTRY
THAT IS SEIZING MEN IN THIS GENERATION. BROTHER REX
WILL CALL MANY PEOPLE FROM THE CONGREGATION, BY
NAME, ADDRESS OR PHONE NUMBER AS HE MINISTERS, TO
PEOPLE AS LED BY THE SPIRIT OF GOD.

You Can't Afford to Miss One of
These Services –

Get Acquainted with Pastor Paul Christian
A man of great faith who will bless your soul. Brother Paul is
compassionate and understands human problems ... feel free
to contact Brother Paul at anytime — Phone 252-6680

REVIVAL

CHRIST CATHEDRAL
Eastern Theatre - East Main St.
COLUMBUS, OHIO

HEAVEN ON EARTH!
thru NOV. 5th

LOCATION:
: Hi Auditorium
MISON AVENUE -
E NIGHTLY – 7:30 P.M.

f's ministry, people are
S, BLINDNESS, CANCER
ness. This is Your Revival
ne . . . God will heal you.

gospel singing
thrill your soul

G. W. DeLatte

Dece HEALING REVIVAL

7:4

2 SERVICES DAILY — 10:30 A.M. & 7:45 P.M.
—FOR ALL PEOPLE OF ALL CHURCHES —

will

NEW LOCATION: SEATING 1100—AIR CONDITIONED

CHRIST CATHEDRAL
1336 E. MAIN ST. COLUMBUS, OHIO
(FORMERLY NEW MAIN THEATRE)

C. B. ELLIS, EVANGELIST

LOCATION:
1624 E. MAIN ST
EASTERN AUDITORIUM

SPECIAL 2:30 P.M.
SUNDAY SERVICE

Prayer for
the Sick in
Every Service

BEGINNING:
FRIDAY, JULY 29th
10:30 A.M & 7:45 P.M.

Preaching - Music -
Come See Hear
The Miraculous Powe

COMING TO

COLUMBUS, OHIO

Samples of handbills.

(Thomas Simson)

**Absent healing:
Prayer cloths and
prayer requests.**
(Thomas Simson)

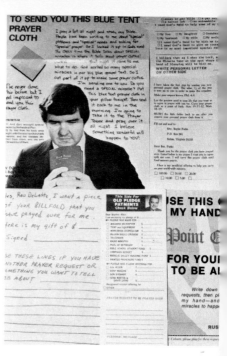

Various journals.
(Thomas Simson)

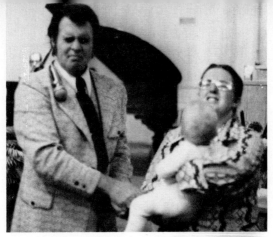

Paul Wells, healing a child with a club foot. Wells said the mother later took the child to a doctor to confirm the healing.

(Paul Wells)

Shannon Johnson, crippled from birth, shown standing without braces (left), and pushing his own wheelchair (right).

(Paul Wells)

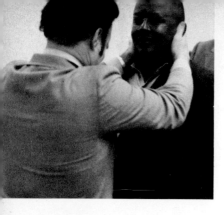

Paul Wells healing
Moses Gatson of his
deafness.

(Paul Wells)

Gatson proclaiming his joy on being able to hear.

(Paul Wells)

Printed in U.S.A.

from visiting his son and that there ensued an angry exchange of words with the hospital personnel. Rev. Hart told his wife: "I'm goin' back out for a while. They say we can't pray for Ralph here or in any hospital, so I'm takin' him home. Some of the members are already there praying. I'll be back as quick as I can."[170]

Leaving his sobbing wife at the hospital, the father headed to one of the local funeral homes and pounded on the door till he awakened the proprietor. Eventually the distraught father was able to obtain an ambulance with which he schemed to take his son from the hospital.

At this stage the parents' main concern, as they later admitted, was not so much with Ralph's life but rather with his heart—whether it was right with God.

At the hospital, flashbulbs were popping, and one question after another was fired at the parents as they carried their son to the waiting ambulance. The reporters noted that the boy was delirious and writhing in pain. When the ambulance reached the Hart home, crowds had already formed to await their arrival. Most of the onlookers were curiosity seekers. Many were in a highly antagonistic mood, calling the parents by nasty names and making sarcastic remarks about them. The early news broadcasts were carrying the story of the "crackpot preacher," who was letting his son die without any medical treatment.

Inside the house they were met by members of their church, who had gathered there to pray. A reporter who gained access to the house later testified that the youth lay on the bed surrounded by weeping men and women.

The father was kneeling by Ralph's side, imploring God to save his son's life.

Tense moments passed. The faithful prayed on the inside while the unbelievers milled around the house on the outside. After a while the father announced that he would permit a surgeon to set the broken collar bone, but would not permit any other kind of medical aid.

113

Pressure was placed on the various full-gospel pastors to take a stand against the Harts, as a wave of criticism swept over the city concerning faith healing. These pastors declared to the news media that sinners always need a physician and there are times when even saved people might need a doctor. They explained that while full-gospel belief includes divine healing, the use of physicians is not really banned. These pastors urged the father to take his son back to the hospital for the recommended medical treatment, but he steadfastly refused to comply with their request. In spite of the pressures, the Hart family continued to place their faith in divine healing as the medium for healing Ralph.

On motion by the county juvenile officer, the court instructed the city health director to ascertain that Ralph was visited at his home several times a day by a physician, who was to be given authority to remove the ailing boy to a hospital and make another spinal puncture if he felt it to be necessary. Ralph himself had actually requested medical aid and had all along fully cooperated with the physicians. However, once he had completely recovered, he credited God with his healing.

More than a year passed. One day his younger brother, 13-year-old Billy Joe, was injured when he rode his bicycle through a red light into the side of a car. He suffered a fractured skull, a fractured hand, and back injuries. He was taken to a hospital, where he was given emergency treatment. As his parents were notified of Billy Joe's condition, there was a repetition of what had occurred when Ralph had been hospitalized. The Harts called a private ambulance and took Billy Joe home against all medical advice. A court order was obtained shortly thereafter to remove Billy Joe from his home and take him back to the hospital. The father, reinforced by sympathetic supporters, refused to allow the police to carry out the order to place Billy Joe under medical supervision. Unable to prevail against the throng of people, the officers were forced to call for additional reinforcements to deal with the situation. A riot appeared imminent as 20 policemen overpowered the parents and a praying crowd, ready to put up a determined fight. While the father was held down forcefully by the police, he rebuked some members of his family and followers who engaged in unkind name-calling of the officers. He implored them to be good Christians and to be above such meaningless, immature acts. As Rev. Hart's eight children—two daughters and six sons—grew up, five of the sons, including Ralph and Billy Joe, followed in his footsteps and became deliverance evangelists.

The parents of Ralph and Billy Joe apparently quite sincerely believed that they should rely on God and prayer, not on worldly physicians, to bring about the healing of their sons. This is what the father had been preaching to his congregation.

Organized Religion While the challenges of the evangelists' doctrines have been most noticeable in the area of scientific medicine, many other ways of the greater society have also become targets of their attack. One of these targets has been the religious life of Americans.

Organized churches have come under repeated attack. They have been accused of being lifeless, indifferent to the spiritual needs of the people, overrigid and secularized, and paying regular salaries to ministers. (NOTE: some evangelists, such as Oral Roberts and Kathryn Kuhlman, also started drawing a fixed income later on in their careers.) It has been pointed out more than once that the churches' activities may be not only ineffective but actually harmful.

"You can get your pornography direct from church," complained Don Stewart. "From a frighteningly growing number of pulpits, sex outside the marriage vows is being preached. Another large major

denomination not long ago put its stamp of approval
on this new morality."[171]

At the revival meetings of a number of evangelists I
witnessed vehement diatribes and execrations directed
against the Roman Catholic Church. On many occasions irreverent remarks were made concerning the pope,
the nuns, and the church's rituals and doctrines.
Pamphlets with such titles as "I Was A Roman Catholic," "The Roman Catholic Plan to Rule the World,"
and "Deliverance from the Heresies of Rome" were distributed. At one revival I heard the evangelist relate
stories of how the priests in Latin American countries
were supposedly torturing and murdering innocent Pentecostal victims. Since the expansion of the charismatic
movement within the Roman Catholic Church, I have
noticed an eclipse or at least a definite softening of
animosities towards Catholics as well as other denominations in the sermons of some of the very same evangelists.

Not all religious groups whose beliefs and practices
differ from their own ministry have come under repeated attack. One such group are the Jews for whom
the evangelists generally have had a great deal of empa-
thy and have frequently pointed out the atrocities that
have been committed against them. During the Middle
East crisis they took a definite pro-Israel stand, con-
demning not so much the Arab people but, rather, their
leaders:

> Although one can have no sympathy for the war-mad
> Arab leaders, we have a deep feeling for the Arab
> people and sympathize with them in their suffer-
> ing.[172]

Race Relations Historically, many faith-healing cults,
particularly the deliverance evangelists, have been promoting equality of people of all races. Racism is contrary

to the Christian doctrine as interpreted by the evangelists. Many early evangelists crusaded against such practices as racially separate seating of people at religious services. For their efforts they were at times tarred and feathered or run out of town by the Ku Klux Klan or other racists groups. These harassments have continued, though they have have lost most of their zeal over the past 10 years.

One of these outbreaks of violence was reported in the 1960s by Atlanta newspapers. There the local Ku Klux Klan disrupted Leroy Jenkins' campaign, ruined his tent with acid, and were able to force him to leave town because of his stand on racial integration. Jenkins gave the following account of this event:

On the Saturday night before we were to close, five men came into the service, but left without causing any trouble. The next afternoon before the service was to start liquid acid dropped down on the benches and organ. We decided to have service anyway. We gathered newspapers together and put them on the benches. We wiped the organ and started the service.

Several members of the Ku Klux Klan came and gathered around. They were giving signals by lighting cigarettes. We could see them through the tent. I started singing "He's Got the Whole World in His Hands." I picked up a little colored baby and sang. . . .

Before the service started I had told the organist, "You go with my wife after service in our car. I will take your car." The organ wasn't hurt by the acid, so we put it in the back of our car.

About the close of the service they lit their cigarettes. I handed the mike over to Charles Sanford and walked out through the side of the tent. I got into my organist's car and drove away. Brother Sanford finished and closed the service. My wife drove away in our Cadillac. Some Ku Klux Klansmen stopped the

car to see if I was there, but they didn't find me.
They didn't see me get into the other car and drive
off because God protected me. They hunted for me
everywhere. I had gone to a motel.[173]

In spite of occasional setbacks suffered by the evangelists for their views on race, they have continued to
attact integrated audiences (though the actual percentage of blacks varies considerably from one evangelist to
another), have an integrated staff, and emphasize the
brotherhood of man. Thomas Wyatt was vocal in
preaching against racial discrimination, colonialism, and
the practice of using natives as servants of whites.[174] St.
Paul Shaver stated:

. . . a man tried to get me to join the Ku Klux Klan.
I said, not me, mister. He asked why not, and I said
they are of the devil, and they have to cover up their
faces because they are afraid and ashamed. So I told
him to shut up. After that he never asked me again,
and I still say they are of the devil, same as the black
shirts, Commies, Nazis, Moslems, and all sinful people.[175]

While the evangelists have expressed apparent concern for the racial situation, they have generally refrained
from supporting the various civil rights movements
and protest demonstrations. They feel that laws as
well as other coercive methods are ineffective in
changing the attitudes of whites towards blacks and
have proposed their own means for dealing with this
persistent social problem. Oral Roberts stated that two
peoples—the Jews and the Negroes—have been the victims of more mistreatment and racial bias than any
other in modern history. He pointed out that there are
other ways of killing people than with guns—it can be
done with "prejudice, hate, name-calling or avoidance."
He warned the whites not to erect a wall against Negroes
and thus kill their spirit, emphasizing that an important

factor in reducing racial tension is for people to get to
know each other and to do things together.[176] W. V.
Grant felt that with patience and effort race relations
can be improved much more effectively through education, which emphasizes that all mankind is created
equal in the sight of God, than through punitive mea-
sures.[177]

A. Wallace, a Negro evangelist, felt that the real solution to the racial problem is for people to turn to
Christ:

> Since men have tried "civil legislation, civil dis-
> obedience, sit-ins, boycotts, walk-outs, protest
> marches, riots, revolutions, racism, law and order in-
> stead of law and justice, de facto segregation, and na-
> tionalistic separation," why not try and accept the
> only real hope we have left, Jesus Christ?[178]

Consensus exists that if only people would turn to Jesus, racism as well as other social problems could be
solved.

Socio-political Scene   Another area of concern has
been much of what is occurring in the socio-political
area. The U. S. Supreme Court has been singled out in
particular as inimical to the Christian way of life. Overwhelmingly, the evangelists have objected to the court's
decisions to outlaw prayers in school and to legalize
pornography. W. V. Grant protested:

> Deadly alcohol, pornographic literature, nude maga-
> zines, nudists camps, adultery, topless waitresses, and
> topless bathing suits are legal in many places. It is
> legal to teach that God is dead, but illegal to pray or
> read the Bible to our children in the schools.[179]

> If a groceryman sells poison food that kills your chil-
> dren, he will go to prison. Yet in front of his store he
> sells poison literature, which poisons the soul, mind,

and spirit of your boys and girls. . . . Eighty-five percent of what we learn comes by reading. Yet in the same day the Supreme Court took prayer and Bibles out of schools, they made obscene literature legal.[180]

Movies, dancing, drinking, and smoking have, among other worldly activities, been denounced as undesirable activities. W. V. Grant observed:

We have pure food laws. Why can't we have pure air laws? Why are we forced to breathe cancerous smoke after it has been sucked down into diseased lungs and blown into our face?[181]

When the peace groups were active, they also were subjected to criticisms. Evangelists claimed, among other things, that these groups were promoting the anti-Christian symbol of the broken cross which used to be known as either the "Crow's Foot" or the "Witches' Foot" during the Middle Ages. According to Bud Chambers:

The Peace Symbol . . . is used today as a central part of the national symbolism of Communist Russia. It appears the Communists are winning their battle for the minds of our youth. They are making special efforts to capture the attention of today's youth in America.[182]

Communists and fellow travelers have often been criticized and their dangers enumerated. Several evangelists have maintained that they have been targets of Communists' hostility and harassment.

"The communists are really after me. They are so afraid of my work. The other day two of them came down to watch us, sat here for a while, and then left. They'll be back. My ministry is in real danger, but God is with me. I promise you all that I will continue even if

I have to fight the commies tooth and nail," declared an obscure evangelist to a crowd of less than 20 souls who had gathered to listen to him at a little, dilapidated storefront church.

While these claims may be dismissed as manipulations of the emotions of the congregation, these feelings of antagonism are not quite without foundation. Pentecostalism, which began to expand in Russia after the revolution of 1917, has been viewed by the Communist Party as a dangerously fanatical movement, and the believers have been accused of being traitors. During Khrushchev's regime many Pentecostals were sentenced to prison terms. The Russian press, says J. T. Nichols in Pentecostalism, has continued to brand them as "criminals and hooligans who indulge in debauchery . . . who alienate the youth from Soviet life, and who are hostile to the State, army, Party, trade unions, and the educational system." When Oral Roberts went to Estonia, he found that it was illegal to bring in Bibles and against the law to speak in tongues. Even prayer meetings had to be held in secret.[183]

These views of the evangelists regarding the state of affairs of the greater society, whether on race relations, worldly pleasures, social problems, or the churches, may well reflect not only their attitudes but also those of their followers. To keep their ministry solvent, the evangelists find it necessary to be tuned in to the expectations and world view of potential converts. One evangelist reported that when he tried to preach the social gospel, he met hostility and rejection from the congregations and cancellations of future preaching engagements.[184] Thus the evangelists have to take at least some care that they express sentiments that will not alienate the kind of followers who are attracted to their brand of religious expression.

Chapter 6

Those Who Follow

From the frontier era to the present day a segment of the American population has continued to search for a meaningful religious experience at the full-gospel revival meetings. It is from among these people that the typical deliverance evangelist draws supporters for his ministry. They become his followers, the true believers who attempt to follow his teachings to the best of their inclination and ability. They are the ones upon whom the evangelist depends for his livelihood, the continuation of his work, and support for the beliefs and values he espouses.

Liz was one of these believers. She was a serious, gaunt-looking woman in her early thirties and had lived most of her life in various cities in Pennsylvania and New York.

My parents were Quakers. They were very religious, but they could not get along with each other. They were always bickering. Mother said that the greatest mistake she ever made was to marry father. I don't know how, but mother started attending Pentecostal meetings. I remember as a kid I was real happy everytime we went to one of those meetings. There was singing, and everybody was so happy and having a good time.

Now Liz is the mother of two children and married to a truck driver who is away from home a great deal of the time.

> My husband does not attend church much. When he is home he usually goes down to the bar or plays poker. I don't see much of him. Someday I hope he gets saved. I pray for his soul all the time.

Liz still looks forward to attending revival meetings just as she did in her childhood.

> They still have revivals like when I was a kid. Only people seemed much closer to each other then. Sometimes I go to several meetings a week, depending on the evangelist and if it is close by. I feel much better afterwards.

She began to have a tight feeling and periodic pains in her stomach.

> I joined the healing line at church, and I was instantly cured. Whenever someone is ill in our family, I pray for them. It's the best medicine. . . . Yes, I have gone to doctors. One time was when my little girl broke her leg. . . . They can help some, but I don't think they can do too much. I always try prayer first.

The place of worship she most frequently attended was Full Gospel Tabernacle, a revival center not too far from her home.

The neighborhood where the Full Gospel Tabernacle was located was familiar grounds to me. My parents and I had lived for many years just a few blocks from this center. I had attended movies there before it became a church. Afterwards I continued to visit it to observe the proceedings and interview the people, such as Liz and Mrs. Cochran, as part of my investigation not only of the evangelists but also of the kinds of people who attend the revival meetings and why they might be attracted to this form of worship.

Social Characteristics of the True Believers: Deliverance Evangelism and the Lower Classes

At the Full Gospel Tabernacle evangelists from all over the country came to hold revivals, sometimes staying for a week, sometimes longer. Though many of these evangelists were obscure, small-time preachers who came and went and I never heard of them again, now and then evangelists well known on the gospel circuit did make appearances and prayed for the sick.

The Full Gospel Tabernacle was located in an old movie theater that had been converted to accommodate nomadic preachers of the Gospel as well as the regular worshipers at the Sunday morning services. It was about a 10-minute drive from the center of a large midwestern city. Years earlier its immediate neighborhood had been a quiet, white, middle-class residential area. As the Negroes—many of whom had been forcibly displaced from another part of the town which had been razed to make way for luxury apartment houses, a freeway, and empty lots on which now weeds grew—started to move in, the whites retreated towards the suburbs till this neighborhood became largely made up of blacks. Some migrants from the Appalachian regions and other poor whites also drifted to this area. As part of these transitions the crime rates started to soar, and signs of decay and slothfulness became increasingly visible.

In these surroundings the Full Gospel Tabernacle originated in the mid-1960s. Over the years it continued to draw much of its support from nearby residents. As the time for the advertised beginning of the revival meeting neared, people could be seen leisurely converging from all directions on this gospel center, whose doors had been thrown wide open as an informal sign of welcome.

Those entering the revival center were both young and old, black and white. Among them were many married women tugging their squirming offspring, whose gleeful shouts echoed through the auditorium. The mode of dress was casual, yet neat—the men in overalls and plaid shirts, the women in cotton housedresses or skirts and sweaters. Only on rare occasions did someone in formal attire make an appearance. These believers were neither wealthy nor well-educated, but they appeared to me to be relaxed and happy there. Overall the audience left the impression of being less affluent than those at the large healing campaigns held in tents on the fairgrounds of the same city. No professional people or even moderately well-to-do individuals ever became regular patrons of this little gospel center.

Historically deliverance evangelism has attracted primarily people not too unlike those at the Full Gospel Tabernacle. In trying to explain why this form of religious expression is particularly attractive to the lower and working classes, Boisen proposed that there exists a definite relationship between economic distress and religious expression. He has maintained that the adherence to Holiness doctrines represents spontaneous attempts on the part of the common people to deal with the stresses and difficulties they encounter.[185] From his investigation, Elinson concluded that the ministry of deliverance evangelists such as A. A. Allen represents primarily a religious solution to the problems of illness, poverty, and lack of status among one's fellowmen.[186] The whole atmosphere of the revival meetings has continued to project certain characteristics, such as emotionality, informality, anti-intellectualism, to mention some of them, which tend to alienate the upper classes, but which many times are particularly appealing to other classes.

Though deliverance evangelism originated in humble

surroundings, the trend in this country has been towards a narrowing of the socio-economic gap between the believers and the rest of society. Marjoe Gortner, among others, observed that the followers, though holding the same belief as in the past, are now better educated than some 20 years ago.[187] While many of the obscure and less well-known evangelists may continue to depend entirely on lower classes for support, such figures as Oral Roberts and Kathryn Kuhlman have drawn crowds that seemed to be not too different from a cross-section of Americans, with many in their audience appearing prosperous and expensively attired. Even several celebrities, such as Joe Louis and Pat Boone, have received solace at revival meetings. One woman at one of the small storefront revivals was reported as saying that she did not care to go to any of Kuhlman's revivals because Kuhlman ministers to the "upper-class whites."

Membership in Voluntary Associations

Despite the fact that the members of the Full Gospel Tabernacle were in the lower income brackets of this country, they managed to be very generous with their hard-earned money. They contributed financially not only to the evangelist but also to other charitable enterprises, such as relief for orphans in Africa. Though they exhibited sincere concerns towards their fellowman and readily gave to what they felt were worthy causes, they themselves were not active in any voluntary associations or movements other than their religion and labor unions. A study of a Southern community revealed that the Pentecostal groups actually discouraged their members from joining voluntary associations with the exception of labor unions.[188] Another study revealed that the teachings of evangelists such as A. A. Allen encourage withdrawal from political activities.[189] The believers at the Full Gospel Tabernacle tended to passively support the Democratic party. I encountered no one who was actively partaking in political matters. This relative lack of involvement is also a further reflection of their class-culture. Research studies have demonstrated that the lower the socio-economic level, the lower the percentage of persons active in voluntary associations, including affiliations with an organized church.[190]

Women

Religious bodies in general, and those involving faith healing in particular, have included an overrepresentation of women. This also holds for deliverance evangelism. At the Full Gospel Tabernacle and nearby tent revivals women were observed to constitute 60 to 75 percent of the audience.

Some have claimed that especially deliverance evangelism is compatible with the problems and temperament of women. Its attraction to women might be explained by the different sex role expectations which allow women more freedom in emotional and nonrational activities or as a reaction to the minority status to which they have been relegated. Revival meetings provide one of the few opportunities available for spontaneous self-expression for women with limited means and education who live in isolated rural areas or violent inner-city neighborhoods. One theory holds that overall women in the United States are more religious than men because their social roles get little reinforcement from secular values. Instead, they must turn to the church for support. The men more often have a place in the secular society, and, therefore, they need less nonsecular support.[191] In particular, the need of religion for elderly women has been emphasized. One authority concluded:

Some elderly men turn to religion in a passionate excessive manner that seems less a spiritual search than a way of filling the void of their former family. If a man is not available, then perhaps a masculine God-figure may give some sense of comfort and meaningfulness. Religion can be truly beneficial, but it can also serve as a cover-up for terribly lonely women who have no relevant human beings in their lives.[192]

The Elderly

Another category of individuals that are welcomed at the revival meetings are the elderly. While at the Full Gospel Tabernacle less than 10 percent of the congregation could be labeled elderly, the age composition of the believers nationally has been reported to form a quite different pattern. Several observers have concluded that an overrepresentation of the elderly exists at the revival meetings. Before retiring from his healing ministry, Oral Roberts commented that though many children and teenagers attended his revivals, more than half of his audience was composed of people over 50.[193]

That deliverance evangelism might be attractive to some of the elderly Americans can well be inferred from the experiences and problems they encounter. The elderly have been increasingly devalued in our materialistic culture, where in essence they are relegated to the status of human obsolescence. They have been forced into retirement, though they may still be capable of handling their jobs adequately, and cajoled to live in segregated developments where they tend to become withdrawn from society. Employers discriminate flagrantly against them and so do many of the health and welfare agencies. A negative stereotype of the aged has been implanted so firmly into the minds of the citizenry that it has even become accepted by the elderly themselves as part of their self-concept, and, though once baseless, it has become a self-fulfilling prophecy. Within religious bodies they have been able to regain some of their lost personal dignity and meaning in life.

As the elderly have had to relinquish involvement with secular pursuits, the importance of religious activities might have grown as a compensation for what they have lost. Studies have shown that more older people are members of religious bodies than of any other kind of voluntary association.[194] It is in the churches more than anywhere else, with the exception of the family group, that the aged have reportedly found personal friendships and other resources to alleviate their loneliness and anxieties.[195] The revival meetings constitute one of the places where they find acceptance and where they can partake of the proceedings according to their desires and abilities no matter how far advanced in age. At the Full Gospel Tabernacle they were accorded equal welcome with the more youthful members and the saving of their souls was seen as just as important as anyone else's.

Possibly of much greater attraction to the elderly has been the attention of the deliverance evangelists have given to the treatment of physical ailments. Though the stereotype of the aged as beset by disabling ailments has been radically exaggerated, an increasing concern in maintaining and restoring health does appear to occur among the aged.[196] Tendencies towards hypochondria, largely among elderly women, have been reported.[197] With retirements and loss of other relevant past activities and the accompanying increase in leisure time, they start paying more attention to normal aches and pains and are likely to blow them out of proportion.[198] At the same time the elderly believe, with more than just a little justification, that physicians are not really concerned about their health problems.[199] All these factors combine to account for the observation that the elderly are frequent contributors to faith healers.[200]

Over the past decade it has been the young people

that have increasingly become involved with various cults,[201] including select fundamentalist groups that promote faith healing. A possible explanation for this trend is that it represents a way of coping and reacting to the spread of family breakdown, absence of meaningful community life, or the proliferation of predictions of disasters of all kinds for mankind in the near future.

Influenced particularly by the popularity of the Jesus movement, efforts have been made by some of the evangelists to reach the young people. A variety of approaches have been utilized for this purpose, such as projecting a more mod image and dealing with drug abuse and other issues especially relevant to the young. One of the evangelists who has made significant changes in his ministry to appeal to the young people is the dynamic H. Richard Hall, who has been a full-time evangelist since 1952. Among others, he successfully recruited a number of highly effective college students to campaign with him. His ability to relate both to his old-time Pentecostal followers and to the youth from the Jesus movement has been considered a remarkable accomplishment.[202]

Black Believers

Besides involving many elderly, women and lower-middle and working-class members, deliverance evangelism also attract a relatively large number of blacks. At the Full Gospel Tabernacle and nearby tent revivals that I attended, the percentage of blacks in the congregation fluctuated greatly, ranging from 15 to 70 percent. Black women were especially prominent, making up 70 to 88 percent of their racial group. Morris observed that towards the end of the 1950s scores of independent faith healers were ministering to congregations that were overwhelmingly black.[203] Due to the historical background, class-culture membership, and personality structure of black Americans, this form of religious expression continues to be suited to a select segment of them.

Over the years the extensive migration of Southern Negroes to the North has infused the popularity of the storefront church revivals into the Northern Negro ghettos. In these small congregations they can worship in a manner to which they have become accustomed and form informal relationships with the other worshipers. Many of the migrants and other lower-class Negroes do not like the large city churches, where they often lose their sense of identity and lack opportunity for meaningful participation. There have been complaints, particularly from the Southern migrants, that neither the congregation nor the pastor knew them personally, and the only recognition they get is as a number on the envelope in which they place their dues.[204]

Generally members of the black storefront churches have no great difficulty adjusting to the ministration of the typical deliverance evangelist since many similarities exist in doctrine and in ecstatic experiences. Marjoe Gortner ended up preaching to more black than white churches and felt that not too many other whites have had this honor.[205] Particularly for the past 15 to 20 years, according to Morris, some of the lesser-known white faith healers have planned their revivals exclusively for Negroes, holding their campaigns in various urban ghettos.[206]

Furthermore, Pentecostalism has been relatively free from racial discrimination from its inception on and has included notable blacks in its leadership. Many cases have been reported where the deliverance evangelists have fought Jim Crowism and, insisting on the brotherhood of all Christians, have tried to assure that at least at the revival meetings a Negro can find equal acceptance.

Elinson observed that the literal interpretation of the Bible and emphasis on spiritual criteria of personal worth has resulted among the followers of such evangelists as A. A. Allen in strong opposition on strictly religious grounds to racial discrimination.[207] At the Full Gospel Tabernacle the whites interviewed expressed their opposition to racial discrimination and segregation and emphasized that it was morally wrong to judge a person on the basis of his race. The consensus was that not by demonstrations or force but only by promoting total commitment to Jesus can racial conflicts and hatreds be eliminated. At least on the surface, these people appear to have been more successful in forming harmonious relationships with people of other races than many other segments of the nation.

Select Observations Among American Indians

It has been proposed that the old-time religious revivals develop and expand under conditions of personal isolation and insecurity incidental to migration and social discrimination.[208] Thus, it is not surprising that some inroads are being made by the deliverance evangelists not only among the blacks but also among Puerto Ricans, Mexicans, and American Indians.

American Indians have increasingly begun to use not only white man's medicine but also white man's faith healing, with Apaches, Navahos, Utes, and other Indians having been exposed to deliverance evangelists. They have received special attention from Oral Roberts, A. A. Allen, and others.

Among the Western Apaches the old-time religion was introduced in the late 1950s, when a number of deliverance evangelists began to hold revivals in Cibecue, a small settlement on the Fort Apache Indian Reservation in east-central Arizona.[209]

Before that time most of these Apaches who attended Christian services continued to adhere to certain native ceremonials and beliefs, particularly to those dealing with curing, because the white man's religion that had been introduced to them made no effective provision for the treatment of sickness. While the missionaries perceived their own brand of Christianity and the religious system of the Indians as diametrically opposed, the Apaches saw nothing contradictory about participating in them simultaneously since there were benefits to be derived from both. Then came faith healers who preached that Jesus could heal all of their ills. Some of these evangelists were Western Apaches themselves. Though they were highly acculturated to the ways of the white man, they proved to be very effective in proselytizing. They could speak the local dialect and were perceived as one of their own kind by their fellow tribesmen who listened silently to tales of personal cures by Jesus. Furthermore, receiving healing at the hands of these evangelists would not require the expenses associated with the Apache native healing ceremonials, and the sick and destitute are spared the worry of making payments. To receive a successful cure, the Indians were told by the evangelists, they not only had to have faith, but also had to renounce their medicine men and stop participating in the traditional ceremonies. The proselytizing efforts were particularly successful among the most acculturated individuals, those who had been marginal Christians but were dissatisfied with its lack of emphasis on curing and those who had serious doubts about the effectiveness of their own medicine men. The conservative Apaches who tried to preserve their traditional ways remained, in contrast, skeptical as to the ability and sincerity of these evangelists. Today the native religious patterns still persist, but their hold on the Cibecue Apaches has been undermined by the deliverance evangelists' emphasis on God's ability to perform miracles and their persistent disparagement of the old ways.[210]

Groups that promote the old-time religion have been established on Apache and Navaho reservations, according to reports published by the various deliverance evangelists, and Indian Pentecostal preachers can be found working among their people in Washington, Montana, and other states.

Place of Residence and Mobility

Though increased mobility and mass communication have had an homogenizing effect on this country, regional variability as to the popularity of faith healing has continued. The average deliverance evangelist can expect better success in Tulsa, for example, than in Boston. Gaines stated that the only part of the country where Marjoe had not preached by the time he reached the peak of his childhood career was New England. The reason for this was that his type of evangelism was not at all popular in that part of the country.[211]

In some regions of this country, owing to their geographical isolation or for historical reasons, certain religious systems have become embedded which are quite compatible with a number of faith-healing practices presently in existence. In other regions the sociocultural environment makes demands on individuals that at least indirectly move them toward the folds of a faith healer. Still other regions attract the kind of migrants who are particularly susceptible to the off-beat and the mystic. One such region which embodies all of the above is the West Coast. California, and especially Los Angeles, has long had an exceptionally high concentration of religions and philosophies as well as plain frauds and quackeries that concern themselves with health problems. There a wide array of esoteric cults and sects, along with many deliverance evangelists have found a lucrative business. There Aimee McPherson achieved great fame and built her temple, O. L. Jaggers instituted his illustrated sermons, and Evelyn Wyatt established Wings of Healing.

A major reason for their success in the Golden State

is that that area has had a constant influx of migrants that have brought with them the problems arising from rootlessness and maladjustment that result from difficulties in coping with a new environment. There are the frustrated individuals who failed to achieve the success they dreamed of, there are the lonely who are far from kin and friends, and there are the deviants who have left their home communities in search of anonymity and new excitements. In the cults they recapture some sense of belonging and assurance which is denied to them by the secular society and the established churches. In response to the repeated question "Why California?" one observer profoundly stated:

. . . Los Angles has attracted, in the years of her phenomenal expansion, a special type of citizenry which the years of depression had rapidly stratified into thick layers of futile, humble, yet anxiously expectant respectability. . . . They were "naturals" for the innumerable cults and sects which narcotized the pangs of their thwarted hopes.

In Los Angeles, too, it was hard to forget the ignominy of failure because one's eyes were so constantly assailed by the arrogant pagentry of success. You dwelt, as it were, on the lowest slopes of the Olympus of Hollywood; and the Gods and Goddesses of that two-dimensional paradise sometimes descended among mortals in their chariots of gold, displaying, competitively and conspicuously, the prizes of their popularity. Prosperity, like everything else, was conceived in terms of pictures; it must be visualized—projected before the eyes of the populace.

Nowhere was the sense of humiliation, of one's utter irrelevance and superfluity in the grandiose scheme of things, rendered more acute than when the crowds gathered to catch a glimpse of the gods and goddesses descending from their cars to attend a "premiere" at some . . . temple . . . . After such fleeting glimpses it was easy, almost necessary, to re-

turn to the anesthetics of . . . [the cults] to deaden
the sting of one's own defeat.

The standing army of "extras" in life drifted in the
direction of any symbol which promised eternal salvation and security.[212]

Another look at the popularity of faith-healing practices in California shows that early in its history the development of medical science was greatly retarded in
that part of the country. This vacuum was filled by faith
healers and other unorthodox practitioners. In addition,
many of the new residents suffered from chronic disabilities or psychosomatic ailments, having often been
advised to move West for their health. Thus faith healing was able to gain early in the growth of that area a
strong foothold and establish a tradition for the most
part in the southern part of the state that was to exert
its influence in years to come.[213] According to McWilliams:

> In such an environment it was, of course, foreor-
> dained, that a Messiah would some day emerge. The
> first local Messiah was a poor, uneducated, desper-
> ately ambitious widow by the name of Aimee Semple
> McPherson.[214]

The rootlessness and individualism that have become
a way of life for increasing numbers of Americans as
the population has continued to soar also have led to
frequent change of residence and isolation from family
and friends for many of the believers at the Full Gospel
Tabernacle. Some of them had been small farmers from
the surrounding area who had been forced out of business by the upward spiraling of the cost of living, others
were migrants from the South who had come to this city
in search of honest work they could perform; some had
been displaced by the slum clearance projects that had
in a frenzy mauled away their entire neighborhood; others, because of layoffs, family break ups, or just plain

restlessness, had been drifting from one place to another. As the more mobile of them moved from state to state, one of the few aspects of their lives to have a feel of continuity was their correspondence and periodical meeting up with their favorite evangelist who in his own nomadic existence might before long come to hold a revival not too far from where they had resettled for the moment.

Personality Traits

The wanderings, the rejection, the sense of uncertainty in a complex, rapidly changing world faced by not a few of the congregation of the Full Gospel Tabernacle may well have led them to desire clear-cut, coherent answers about the state of affairs of the universe and eternity and their position in the scheme of things. Though the evangelist readily obliged them with brief explanations, many stresses continued to bother them. All these experiences were bound to leave an imprint on their personality, which in many cases I observed had become introverted, unpretentious, and credulous. They tended to exhibit symptoms of inferiority and guilt complexes as they worried about doing right and begged forgiveness for the sins they had committed. There were signs that they too, as has been found for some Neo-Pentecostals,[215] might have a need for guidance from authority figures and wanted to lean on someone more important and powerful than they.

From recent research it can be inferred that overall they are no more maladjusted psychologically than the rest of society. Some of their behavior, such as glossolalia, are generally not considered symptoms of mental illnesses, but have been interrupted by some as learned behavior.[216,217,218]

A number of them did exhibit, however, what I feel were hypochondric tendencies as they obviously relished to discuss their efforts at "shopping around" for medical care. Their acceptance of faith healing did not completely dissuade many of the believers from seeking medical aid whenever they deemed it necessary. According to their testimonies they appeared quite willing to acquiesce in the physicians' diagnoses and prognoses of their state of health. It was in the area of their general interaction with the physicians and the treatment prescribed by the physicians that a great deal of criticism or even rejection occurred.

While the believers had their share of problems and worries and were expected by their religion to abstain from many of the worldly pleasures, they knew how to have a good time. During the first year that I attended the Full Gospel Tabernacle, I was impressed with the lusty spirit and enthusiasm of the people there. Often the church was more than half filled with shouting, stomping, and handclapping worshipers. During the following years, however, there occurred a near complete turnover in the membership and the attendance dropped noticeably. Day after day only a handful of members showed up. Even a prominent evangelist was unable to draw a decent crowd. The place was fading away, ignored or forgotten by the community.

Deliverance Evangelism and the Needs of the Believers

What happened at the Full Gospel Tabernacle has also happened to the ministry of various evangelists. More than one evangelist built a sizeable following, only to have his followers begin to slip from his grasp with no new converts forthcoming. Eventually he had no choice but to fade from the revival scene.

To keep this from happening to their own ministries, the typical evangelists have found it essential to continually try to stay tuned to the problems and needs of their followers. To do otherwise may well be to risk survival, as some have reported from their experiences. Thus it is by no means just the personality of the evangelists but also to a very significant extent the characteristics of the true believers that determine the nature and direction of deliverance evangelism.

While it may be quite true, as many have claimed, that the major appeal of deliverance evangelism is its involvement with illnesses and disabilities, large numbers of believers are healthy and robust. When asked why they had come to the revival meetings, a number of the believers at the Full Gospel Tabernacle mentioned healing. In far more cases, however, they indicated that they simply desired to partake of a religion that was sacred to them and to worship God in a manner they deem right. Here their beliefs and values receive support and reenforcement and their whole existence is made understandable and worthwhile.

Whether they have come to adhere to this form of religion as a continuation of their childhood training, as the result of a sudden conversion in adulthood, because of concern for bodily ailments, or for other conscious or unconscious factors that may have predisposed them to turn to it, the rank and file followers can have many of their shared needs met at the revival meetings. There is a chance for excitement and release of tensions through mysterious psychic experiences; they find acceptance and enhancement of their sense of worth; meaningful participation and entertainment is provided; and finally they are given hope—hope for a better tomorrow and for the salvation of their soul.

Psychic Experiences At the revival meetings the worshipers can have mind-expanding experiences in the form of trances and glossolalia. They have allegedly had beautiful visions and unforgettable sensations: They have been in the presence of God and His angels, visited heaven, and felt great joy at being alive. Whether

these states are explained as possession by the Holy
Ghost, as the believers do, or as hypnosis or self-
hypnosis, as some scientists that have observed these
behavior patterns do, they do appear to bring about
fantasies very similar to those induced by mescaline and
LSD.[219] Yet they produce none of the negative consequences of the illegal drugs—no laws are broken, no
psychiatric impairment results, and no chromosome
damage is done. Furthermore, these states are highly
sanctioned by the believers' religious community. Thus,
instead of being regarded as odd, as many of their fellow Americans have viewed them, or defined as mentally ill, as some psychiatrists have labeled them, they
receive positive recognition from the rest of the congregation, many of whom themselves undergo similar
psychic adventures. All this constitutes for them further
proof in the reality of an afterlife and the salvation of
one's soul. The dissociation states may also function as
safety valves for pent-up tensions, frustrations, and hostile impulses, and many times leave the participants relaxed with a general sense of well-being and relief.

Self-esteem A positive self-concept, a view of oneself
as a worthwhile individual, is repeatedly promoted. The
worth of every single soul is emphasized, and occasionally sermons revolve around the theme that the born-
again need not feel inferior to anyone. They are told
time and again how Jesus cares about each of them and
that to Him they all are important—just as important as
the very rich and famous, if not more so. Being poor,
old, black, or uneducated is no stigma, for Jesus loves
everyone of His children. In this religious context the
worth of a man is not measured in terms of worldly success, but rather how good a Christian he is. Isn't it stated
in the Bible that in the sight of God all men are equal,
and even the greatest of sinners can find acceptance, if
only they repent and are born again?

To achieve success the members are asked to meet

goals that are realistic most of the time. Being a good
Christian within the framework of "that old-time" religion is not exactly an easy task. It involves not only
adherence to a relatively rigid dogma but also absti-
nence from many worldly pleasures that daily tempt the
believers. Yet the goals are of such a nature that the
individual can conceivably achieve them if he wants to
strongly enough. Thus, within his religious group a dedicated member may be considered a worthwhile, possibly even an outstanding, human being though the secular world has rejected him as a total failure. For a man
can be expected to read the Bible daily, love Jesus, and
abstain from deviant sex acts, alcohol, dirty movies, and
brawls, but no matter how hard he tries and how capable and noble he is, he might never be able to achieve
such secular goals as great wealth, power, and good
looks.

A Sense of Belonging   At least some degree of belonging in a world that provides so little of it is fostered by the
revival meetings as they make available a setting for
like-minded worshipers to come together. The individuals find acceptance as they are—there is no need for
pretense or image building. As long as they are sincere
in respecting the basic religious tenets, they can expect
a warm welcome. The greater society may look down
upon them all and ridicule their mode of worship, but
this only strengthens their solidarity. As the evangelist
preaches on the messages he has received from God, the
significance of his mission, the harassment meted out
by the unbelievers, and visions of the future, those present begin to feel that they are part of a vast and im-
mensely important undertaking. The bond between the
believers may be weak and more spiritual than social,
but there is something to hang on to and to identify
with—a place to go.

Meaningful Participation and Entertainment Revival meetings present various opportunities for participation. Speaking in tongues, going into a trance, volunteering for special prayers, or going up front to be saved are some of them. People can also shout, sing, and dance as the Spirit moves them. Many stand up and testify what God has done for them or tell of some of their problems and transgressions. At least at the smaller revivals nearly everyone who wants to speak up gets the chance to tell his story. These testimonies and confessions of sin may not only reduce inner tensions and guilt feelings but also provide the participants with personal recognition, attention, and publicity.

Evangelists try to make the revival meetings entertaining and joyous affairs—replacements for the many tabooed worldly amusements. There is swinging music and singing, humorous and interesting stories are related, and apparently miraculous healings and other forms of thaumaturgy may be observed. The rejoicing, happiness, and emotionalism that permeate many gatherings can be highly contagious and distract the mind from everyday worries and sorrows. Thus, deliverance evangelism may function as an escapism from the drudgeries and injustices that many of them encounter in their day-to-day existence.

The importance of providing entertainment for the believers is emphasized by Marjoe Gortner, who, in analyzing his role as an evangelist, stated:

> I'm an entertainer for the Lord. I'm an evangelist, not a priest or a holy man. These people come to hear me to forget their miseries for a while, and I've got to give them their money's worth. . . . What they want to hear is what they've heard all their lives. What they want is a good time, a moving experience. . . . these people don't just go to church; they say, "Let's *have* church!" like let's have a party.[220]

143

Hope Finally, the believers are given hope for a better tomorrow to keep them going and prevent discouragements from overwhelming them. Many and vivid are the promises for health, wealth, and happiness that supposedly will be fulfilled for those who have been saved and who continue to follow the dictates of Jesus. And even if these promises fail to materialize on this earth, there surely awaits them a glorious new beginning in the world beyond.

Anxieties and insecurities of life and death are assuaged as they are repeatedly assured that Jesus cares and is concerned over their welfare. God is presented as a kind and forgiving deity, and no matter how great their sins have been, there is still hope for them to receive His blessing. The saving of their souls and receiving eternal salvation is presented as well within their reach.

In other words, the true believers become engulfed in a dream world that provides an escape from the realities and responsibilities of life and at the same time provides bases for feeling morally justified.

Chapter 7

The Others

Americans go to revival meetings for many reasons. True believers attend simply because they have come to accept the version of the Gospel preached by the deliverance evangelists as the only right way to happiness and salvation. For others, the motives for attending range along a broad spectrum from fanatical devotion to violent opposition, with several types in between. There are four major groups—extremists, seekers, observers, and antagonists—each with their own problems and impact on the ministry of the evangelists.

Extremists

Though the true believers are devoted and faithful followers of the evangelist, their religious involvement does not incorporate the singleminded commitment and, at times, bizarre behavior that is exhibited by a group of followers I have labeled as the extremists who represent the fanatical fringe of the following.

Certain extremists go beyond being simply believers to a point at which they overconform to the tenets of their religion. They try to live up to every aspect of the doctrine to a significantly greater extent than is expected of the rank and file followers. One such dedicated soul, a Negro youth in his early teens, was pointed out to me at the Full Gospel Tabernacle by an elderly man: "Bill is more of a Christian than all the people in the state of Ohio put together."

"If only people would accept Jesus, how beautiful life would be. Only through Jesus can we find the way. Jesus can do anything . . . ," Bill testified at one of the revival meetings. He was a likeable, well-built youth who seemed much more mature than others of his age. He talked constantly about God, and whenever he was asked a question he managed to include the mention of Jesus in his replies.

"Every cent he can get hold of he brings to God," one of the women told me.

"I have never met anyone as dedicated as this child, and I have met some pretty good Christians. He is going to make a great preacher and do much for the poor people," added her companion, another woman familiar with the membership of this gospel center.

According to the stories, Bill came from a very disorganized family. His mother had had several common-law marriages, and two of his brothers had been repeatedly in trouble with the police. The boy continued to be a loner, neither much interested in school nor willing to engage in acts of delinquency, until one day, "led by God," as he later testified, he had entered the Full Gospel Tabernacle and found a new life. Now he reportedly offers all he can to the services of the Lord and is admired for his saintlike character.

Besides the overconformists, such as Bill, there are fanatics who in religious zeal exceed the bounds of tolerable behavior. Their interpretations of Biblical statements is of such an extreme nature that they encounter criticisms or even complete rejection from the ordinary believers.

One such case involved an accountant and his wife, who were considered by their neighbors to be a respectable, middle-class couple. Having attended many campaigns conducted by A. J. Valdez Jr., they became convinced that they should pray and fast for three days to force an "outpouring of God." When their seven-year-old foster daughter became exhausted and refused to kneel any longer in prayer for the miracle, the father beat her violently and then strangled her to death. Following the slaying the couple continued to kneel in prayer all night long. Later he told the police that they had punished the girl because she had mocked God. He and his wife were found not guilty by reason of insanity. They were committed to a mental hospital and later released. During their trial Valdez' name was brought into the testimony, and the entire incident provoked strong protests against the evangelist.[221,222]

Extremists can become a source of embarrassment and conflict for the evangelist. Some, such as the Parkers (see Chapter 1), who adhere fanatically to the doctrines, may bring down the wrath of the greater society. Others by their bizarre behavior may lead to ridicule of his ministry by the public and mass media. Occasionally those who engage in practices he rejects have managed to cause turmoil at the meetings. Others of particularly strong convictions and character point out the shortcomings of the evangelist, to his discredit.

Marjoe Gortner has complained about this last aspect. According to Gaines, Marjoe came to recognize certain unpleasant traits in the all-white congregations of the 1970s. He saw them as tending to sniff out scandal even where none existed and holding the preachers' private lives under constant scrutiny, remaining unforgiving to lapses in morals.[223]

Overall, the behavior of the extremists is often blamed on the influence of the evangelist and at times results in greater restrictions imposed by the society on the activities of the evangelist. My investigations left me with the definite impression that at least a number of the evangelists view the extremists with a great deal of ambivalance and not a little amount of apprehension. They would much rather deal with the ordinary believers and their human weaknesses or even with those who are nothing more than seekers.

Seekers

Many come to revival meetings to seek solutions to personal problems. Unlike the true believers, they are not necessarily committed to any extent to, or even familiar with, this form of religious worship. Instead, their attachment to it is rather segmental, limited to the specific condition for which they hope to find a cure.

I met one such seeker at the close of an afternoon revival meeting of a popular evangelist. She was a tall, well-dressed woman who had flown into town with her son for the sole purpose of seeing this faith healer.

"My son is blind," she explained. "It happened recently. He is not used to it. . . . He could never accept it. He has always wanted to be an artist. Studied painting for years. Father had a special studio built for him. Then this. . . . We have seen specialists the world over. They have not been able to help."

She was resigned to the idea that medical science could not help, but was not willing to concede that her son's case was hopeless. She said: "There are so many things that science does not know yet. Maybe the faith healers are our only hope. I don't think he could take it if he thought he would have to be blind all of his life."

That evening the tent was crowded with thousands of people, so I was unable to locate them. It was not until the next morning's revival that I spied them in the sparse audience. They both looked tired and discouraged. They planned to come back for the big healing meeting in the evening and then leave the next day.

The son, a slender, dark-haired youth in his 20s, was in an irritable mood, stating that he certainly was not going to be cured here, while the mother was already reflecting on the various other faith healers they might seek out next to deal with his affliction.

Seekers, such as this mother and her blind son, who come to the revivals are not dedicated supporters of this mode of religious expression nor its precepts, yet they may hope to find some solace and succor for their personal problems. Although their needs may be of a social, psychological, or organic nature, the possibility of receiving healing appears to be the greatest attraction for these seekers.

Besides the incurables or "straw graspers" stricken with terminal illnesses or extreme disabilities, there are those who are suffering from afflictions that are not hopeless but which modern medical science has failed to remedy; consequently some feel compelled to turn to alternative sources. An elderly lady told an acquaintance of mine:

"I had this pain in my back for a long time. I went from one doctor to another, but they didn't do anything for it. Said they couldn't find anything. Half the time I imagine they didn't take me too seriously. A woman at work kept telling me about the revival meetings she goes to and the healings there. I went there then though I'm a Methodist myself. The evangelist prayed for me. I feel better, but the pain still isn't completely gone."

Other seekers of the services of the faith healers consist of tormented individuals suffering from various psychological stresses and traumas. Hoping to find some respite from their mental anguish, they are willing to attend the revival meetings, though they may be uncertain as to the religious significance of the "old-time" religion. One middle-aged woman, for example, started to attend a Pentecostal Church and revival meetings as a consequence of shock caused by the death of her husband.

Possibly one of the more significant contributions of the faith healers lies in the area of ministry to addicts. In view of the ineffectiveness of the costly rehabilitation centers and the contemporary popularity of supernatural and psychic exploration, it is not surprising that at least some who have developed habits detrimental to their welfare seek out deliverance evangelists. Morris, a critic of the ministry of A. A. Allen, had, nevertheless, the following to say about Allen's efforts in this area:

> The Surgeon General's report in 1964 condemned cigarettes and tobacco as a health hazard, and the evangelist promptly started an American Rescue Operation against tobacco, alcohol, and drugs. He was years ahead of most organizations that would later sound an alarm over the scandal of drug abuse. And despite the fact that he integrated the rescue mission with his regular financial plans, this operation, which he continued for a number of years, unquestionably did much good.[224]

Many other evangelists have also made special efforts to seek out the troubled and addicted. They have done this through dissemination of articles and books about their problems and through financial support to certain established social service agencies. For example, Don Stewart has made significant contributions to Youth Action[225] and Paul Wells to WAY-IN home.[226] These agencies try to rehabilitate young people with drug-related or other problems.

Testimonies abound of people who either on their own or through the urging of a kin or acquaintance came to a revival meeting and supposedly were freed from gambling, drinking, smoking, or the use of drugs. I have also heard of those who came and went without any change in their conditions. But their stories have been much more difficult to locate.

The alienated might also detour to the revival meetings. The growing attraction of the "old-time" religion has been explained as possibly a reaction against the growing formality of the major denominations and their failure to meet the spiritual needs of some of their members. For many, particularly members of the more disadvantaged groups, there is also a lack of understandable explanations about the functioning of the society of which they are a part. According to Rose, the diminishing ability of our society to provide satisfactory and convincing explanations of the natural and social events has led to a so-called subjective sense of ignorance. Rose maintains that modern man is better informed than his ancestors, yet has less of a feeling of understanding the world around him, for he is no longer provided with a comprehensive world view, the facts he learns are less integrated and less readily explainable, and with the phenomenal accumulation of information he realizes he can acquaint himself only with a small part of the knowable world around him.[227] A need for simple, understandable answers to the complex events that surround modern man may well lead the seeker to religious bodies and to deliverance evangelists.

I met one such alienated person years ago at a New York coffee shop that was run by a fundamentalist religious group. Life had become somehow meaningless for her. She did not understand what was happening around her; so many things just did not make sense. She appeared to have had no great personal problems, just a vague sense of confusion and desperation. She stated that she had been to some old-time revivals. She did not really believe, but did feel that the people there had something that she was missing.

Occasionally the seekers have proven to be troublesome. There have been cases where they have tried to sue the evangelist or have accused him of medical quackery because their ills were not cured promptly. One evangelist claimed that those unhappy "clients" who complain that they have suffered adversely from his ministration have always been marginal members lacking in proper faith.

For other seekers, however, their loneliness, addiction, and psychosomatic illnesses have been alleviated at the revival meetings. While they do not provide such a dependable support as the true believers, they can be viewed as constituting an important source for future converts. Converted or not, their testimonies can further provide effective publicity as to the efficacy of the ministry of the evangelist—for here are erstwhile skeptics, not blind followers, who came and were healed.

Observers

Another group of people I encountered at the revival meeting were those who were there simply to observe the proceedings. Unlike the seekers, they have no pressing personal problems they hope will be solved there, and unlike the antagonists they have no hostile intentions. Instead they might have come for a professional or academic motive such as that of a neutral reporter covering a story or a student working on a term paper. They may be there in response to the wishes or pleadings of an acquaintance, a friend, or a relative. Or they may simply want to satisfy their curiosity or be entertained by the swinging music and colorful sermons. Some of these observers may come to feel the impact of the revival quite deeply. A Quaker woman stated:

My neighbor always pestered me to go with her to one of these meetings. I was against it, thinking that the people there were a bunch of fanatics. Finally I consented to go with her to see what she saw in it. I went back a second time. During the third time I was saved.

A young Jewish couple decided out of curiosity to attend a revival conducted by C. B. Ellis:

"If anyone had told us that we would be converted I would have told them that they were crazy," testified the wife, "We both come from a very traditional Jewish background, and this sort of thing wasn't for us. Then at the revival we both felt something powerful go through us. I began to tremble and I saw beautiful colors and Jesus was beckoning to me. I'd never felt anything like it before. After we left the meeting we discussed our experience and realized that Jesus was for us. We have not had an opportunity to see Brother Ellis again, but we have been attending Pentecostal prayer groups ever since."

The observers may be covertly welcomed by the evangelist. They add to the size of the crowd, generally prove to be quiet and unobtrusive, at times they contribute financially and some of them may be even converted. Usually they are therefore tolerated and ignored.

Occasionally, however, an evangelist may single them out for harassment or expel them from the meeting. He may resent having nonbelievers seek casual entertainment from something that is sacred to him and his followers. He may mistake them for hostile antagonists, out to compile an exposé on him, or he may just want to create some excitement for the congregation.

One time my mother and a friend of hers were attending a revival meeting to help me compile data for my dissertation. The evangelist started to accuse them of being evil spirits sent by the devil. They left quietly, not bothering to refute his charges.

One problem that the evangelist faces is that some of the observers may be turned into antagonists by their experience. One college student who attended a revival meeting out of curiosity when he had nothing else to do commented afterwards:

"I became appalled at the authoritarian manners of the evangelist and his high pressure tactics to collect money. He was just out to fleece these poor people. There should be a law against it."

153

Antagonists

Some come to revival meetings with a hostile attitude towards the evangelist and his campaign. They are the antagonists. They not only do not believe, but they are also critical of at least that particular deliverance evangelist if not all of them. They make their appearance with the expressed purpose of disrupting the services, vilifying the manner of worship of the believers, or undermining the work and character of the evangelist.

Methods Used by the Antagonists   The methods of attack of the antagonists range from the legal to the illegal, from violent to nonviolent. In their most virulent manifestations, antagonists have resorted to physical violence.

Around the turn of the century mad dogs and drunks played havoc at many a revival, intimidating and pushing around the evangelist and his followers. Beating up the preacher was not uncommon, and sometimes firearms were dangerously discharged into crowds of worshipers. Willis Brown, a 19th-century deliverance evangelist, gave the following account of his most obstreperous meeting:

> They shouted the first night I preached, but the third and fourth nights they did not shout nor amen. God sent the truth so it uncovered sin, and a good many concluded God had not sent me. The professors began to persecute. They got the world stirred against me and the devil howled, but this made no change in the preaching. So the last night of the meeting, just as we presented the altar [call], the pistols began to ringout, to pour in at the windows. The people began to fall on the floor, some knocked down with stones, and some dropped down to keep from getting knocked down. . . . I could not see any . . . on

their feet. . . . One sister who . . . had often said
she could not pray aloud . . . now prayed louder
than any one else. Some of the sinners ran out and
began to shout at the gang, and they ran off. We
prayed for the brother that was hurt worst; God
healed him, and gave victory. Praise God![228]

Contemporary evangelists have also encountered antagonists who were bent on violence. Leroy Jenkins had
his tent and other equipment damaged by the Ku Klux
Klan and was driven out of Atlanta by them. There was
an assassination attempt on Oral Roberts. Later on in
Roberts' career, riots broke out against him in Australia
during which a tent rope was cut, a truck was set on
fire, threats of physical harm were made against him, and
he had to rely on the police to protect him from the
mobs.

From my observations I have concluded that presently only on rare occasions have the antagonists actually used direct physical force. More frequently they
stop short of committing bodily harm and direct their
efforts at disrupting the revivals or suppressing the freedom of speech of the evangelists. This they achieve by
setting off firecrackers, heckling, or shouting threats
and obscenities, or they search the law books for local
ordinances that the evangelist might have violated, or
they try to file a disturbance-of-the-peace charge
against him. During A. A. Allen's British campaigns in
the mid-1960s, for example, he encountered student
demonstrators who picketed his meetings, staged sit-
down protests outside, and disrupted the proceedings inside until they were forcibly removed by the police.

In other conflict situations, the antagonists have tried
in a more orderly manner to point out to the congregation possible errors or inconsistencies in the healer's
work or challenge him to perform specific acts to prove
his claimed power. Gordon Lindsay reported the following disruption of a healing revival:

About midway in the Houston campaign . . . a certain hostile clergyman who opposed Divine healing, denounced the remarks of Rev. F. F. Bosworth . . . and issued a public challenge through the newspapers, to debate with Rev. Bosworth on the subject of "Divine Healing Through the Anointment." Rev. Bosworth felt led to accept the challenge. . . . As the meeting got under way, it was quite apparent that the sympathy of the vast audience was almost entirely on the side of the . . . evangelist.[229]

Still others have been less conspicuous in their antagonism and have tried to work within the structure of the revival meeting to ridicule or expose the evangelist. At a special Holy Ghost Jamboree held in Columbus, Ohio, the evangelist in charge guaranteed instant Holy Ghost to everyone. First he called all the women who were interested to "come and get it." He lined up the interested parties in front of the stage and then went down the line barely touching them, usually simply pointing at each one. All the women fell down on the floor in a trance. To prevent them from hurting themselves another person stood behind them in order to catch them as they collapsed. After a while when most of the women had recovered and returned to their seats, the evangelist called the men to come forward and receive the Holy Ghost. One man who had been highly critical of the healings that had taken place during the previous revivals felt that this was his opportunity to expose the evangelist. With this in mind, he joined the procession of men walking down the aisles to the front of the hall. One after another the men fell into a trance in the same manner that the women had done earlier and lay on the floor. One burly young man standing not too far from the antagonist was the only one not to respond immediately. The evangelist then placed his arm around the man and managed to put him in a trance also. When it was the turn of the antagonist to receive the Holy Ghost, he too fell down like the others.

It was strange. The evangelist barely touched my cheeks. The next thing I know I'm on the floor. I must have been out not much longer than half a minute. I had no particular sensation nor spiritual experience. I was just out. I can't explain how it could have happened. He didn't stare into my eyes, there was no music nor chanting of any kind, and as far as I can tell there were no special gimmicks.

Finally, the largest number of antagonists appear as quiet observers. They are at the revival meetings in order to compile data which later can be used adversely against the evangelist. They may try to ridicule, expose quackery, or warn against the pitfalls of misguided religious enthusiasm and the dangers of faith healing. They may present factual reports or distort their observations to support their own ideological position. Don Stewart complained to me that his ministry had been mocked and misrepresented by the mass media. Other evangelists have voiced similar objections.

Consequences Over the years the numbers and the virulence of the antagonists appears to have been declining. The more successful evangelists employ efficient bouncers to deal with the first signs of possible troublemakers in the crowd before the situation gets out of control. Paradoxically, the hostile actions of the antagonists may be said to both hurt and aid the target of their attack.

Contrary to their own intent, the antagonists can promote the career of the evangelist. They provide him with publicity—and in this day and age public exposure effectively draws potential converts to a movement. They increase his apparent importance. Would an ineffectual and insignificant figure provoke these outbursts? These confrontations add excitement to the revival meeting and provide the evangelist with fresh topics for his sermons. Attacks on the religion itself may lead the followers to seek even closer affinity with him and reaffirm their loyalty to the faith. If the antagonism is severe enough, the evaneglist may emerge as a true martyr who is able to exploit this status by playing on the emotions of his followers.

In spite of this, the antagonists do manage to create much that is detrimental to the evangelist. Being attacked and accused, falsely or not, leads to feelings of anxiety, shame, and apprehension. Hard-to-replace property may be vandalized, and the followers intimidated. The psychological stress curtains the evengelist's ability to function in his private life and his professional capacity. The public concern aroused by the critics limits the extremes to which the evangelist feels he can go without fear of suppression. Through trial and error he and his colleagues have tried to establish boundaries for their ministry that the rest of society is willing to tolerate. In the process they have been forced to relinquish some of their more radical practices and to exercise more caution in what they preach. Above all the antagonists have kept alive over the years a suspicion of fraud and quackery in connection with this ministry. Even some believers have been forced to wonder whether they are saints or charlatans?

The Story of an Antagonist

Together Mr. Cheek and Rev. Stegall sought out Evangelist J——, the former to receive a healing, the latter to prove that J—— could not heal. Here is Rev. Stegall's version of this quest:

. . . I developed a personal interest in an old man I had seen two days before when I dropped in briefly to watch J——at a "great Sunday rally." This man, an old gentleman by the name of Cheek . . . had suffered a stroke . . . and was partially paralyzed in his legs as a result. When the meeting was ending, I found myself blocked behind him, because of his slow

progress up the aisle. He was being helped by his
sister, herself not young . . . . I could not but feel
pity for the old man as he struggled along, pausing
from time to time to breathe heavily. So I put a hand
under him and offered my help, which they gratefully
accepted. . . . I had learned that they lived only a
few miles further than my destination, so I volun-
teered to drive them home. On the trip, I learned that
Mr. Cheek had several times tried to get into the
line, but . . . while he was struggling forward, so
great a line formed that he was unable to get to it.
His faith and that of his sister, that if they could only
get J——to attend to him he would be healed, was
complete. J——that afternoon had stated . . . that
anyone not having been healed should come to Brother
B——'s Church and he would take care of them, with
or without a card. . . . I was fairly well convinced
that the healers were frauds; but I . . . had never
really had a chance to prove them. . . . Here, it
seemed, was a God-given opportunity. . . .

Monday morning I delivered them to the church
despite a downpour . . . only to see the old man
cruelly disappointed when J——called only for those
who "were having severe internal pain, RIGHT
NOW." That let the old man out. . . . Next . . .
J——laid a trap for himself by inviting anyone who
wanted to break a habit—"tobacco, liquor, or women"
—to come forward. Mr. Cheek chewed tobacco, and
now expressed the desire to break the habit. So I led
him forward.

J——came down from the platform and went from
person to person, "healing" them. . . . So I
watched . . . J——, while Mr. Cheek waited, trembling with expectancy, for his glorious moment. It
never came. When all the people were lying on the
floor, J——turned and went back onto the platform.

. . . I went . . . to old Mr. Cheek and stood him
up and started to turn around to take him back to

the pews. Looking up, I saw J——standing at the pulpit, his eyes fixed upon us. Spontaneously, I said, "Mr. J——, this old man had a stroke, and his legs are paralyzed . . ."

J——'s face turned red with anger, and he flashed in a fierce voice, "I know what's wrong with him! I can diagnose any disease!" Completely taken aback, I stammered, "Will you heal him?" "Bring him tonight to the meeting!" said J——and turned on his heel. . . .

. . . Shortly afterwards, B——came to us and said apologetically, "Mr. J——said if you'd bring him tonight and tell him you are there, he'll heal him. He said there wasn't enough Holy Spirit for a big healing like this."

. . . That night . . . talking to B—— I reminded him of the morning's exchange, and he promised to speak to J——about it. . . . This he did, and the word presently came back to me, "Bring him backstage and sit him on the platform in the wings, and when the healing is over, Mr. J——says he will heal him personally." It was a great labor to move the old man through the narrow doors and up the steps . . . but this we did. . . . We waited . . . for the meeting to end. Finally it ended, and we waited with increasing anticipation for the great moment. But as one of the ministers stepped forward to say the benediction, J——slipped out the side and popped into the light-switch booth (which he was using as a dressing room). I called B——and [another man] to me in some anxiety, indicating Cheek. They reassured me that J——would soon be out. I waited, standing. Suddenly, J——popped out again, his clothes changed and made for the darkened exit. He would have been gone before anyone could move a muscle, except that the janitor intervened with a pleasantry. By the time J—— disengaged himself, I was between him and the door and asking him, "Can your heal Mr. Cheek now?"

. . . Sullenly, without meeting my eye, he raised his objections. "Why wasn't he in the healing line? I don't heal without a line. Everybody in the world would want special attention if I healed them individually." . . . I protested, "But you sent word to have him wait here, that you'd heal him specially!"

. . . "Well, I can't heal him tonight. It's too late. Bring him tomorrow night and have him on the healing line, and I'll take him personally then." I asked, to make sure that it was clear, "Even without a card?" J——replied impatiently, "Yes, yes. Put him in the healing line, and I'll take care of him then."

So the third effort came to nothing. . . . The faith of the family in J——had very much decayed during all this, but they still believed that God could heal if they could just get J——to do it. So I promised that I would meet them again next night and we'd try one more time.

The next night we arrived early enough to get a good front seat on the aisle for Mr. Cheek. When the invitation was given for the healing line to form, I assisted him down the aisle to the foot of the steps, and was struggling to get him up the steps when suddenly two burly men seized me by the arms and while one said in my ear, "You don't go any further!", the other took Mr. Cheek and said, "Let's go back to the prayer room." I said, "He's not here for salvation, but for the healing line." They ignored me and tried to pull us apart, at which I balked and jerked my arms loose. "Listen, Mr. J——told me to bring this man!" . . .

Suddenly, as I stood there holding the now-trembling and frightened Mr. Cheek, a hand fell on my shoulder and I was jerked around. Looming over me was the livid face of J——himself. Bellowing into the microphone he shouted passionately, "Get off this platform! Get out of the building! Leave at once, sir!" Astounded, I said, "But you told me to bring this man tonight!" "I did nothing of the sort!" J—— shouted. "Get out of here at once!" I saw that discretion was the better part of research at this point, and was turning to leave, when I thought again of Mr. Cheek. I hoped that he would not be discriminated against on my account, and turned to intercede on his behalf. At that J—went completely insane with rage and bellowed into the microphone, "Call the police! Have this man taken out and thrown into jail!"

I might still have escaped had I run like a terrified dog for the exit. These men are used to having their followers grovel before them. . . . However, I am not used to slinking about, so I walked down the center aisle amid the boos and catcalls of the "Christians." At the end of the aisle a scowling man flashed a badge and informed me that I was under arrest. A mob of people followed us out onto the street, screaming, shouting, and kicking at me.[230]

The case ended in court where the judge gave the antagonist a stern lecture and told him to forfeit his $13 bond.[231] But all this did not deter Rev. Stegall from continuing his mission to try to demonstrate that the deliverance evangelists were indeed charlatans.

Chapter 8

Saints or Charlatans?

There was a hushed silence among the thousands of people crowded under the huge canvas tent as they watched the dark-haired, chubby, 37-year-old Jack Coe minister to yet another one of the many afflicted who sought his help. He placed one hand on the head of a small, polio-stricken, three-year-old boy who was held up to him by the worried mother.

"Jesus, heal this boy," shouted the evangelist.

Hope flushed across the mother's face as he proceeded to command,

"Remove the braces!"

The people who came to this meeting knew that healings were taking place and that nothing was impossible for God. All around them were canes, crutches, and wheelchairs that had been discarded by their former users and now served as constant reminders of the healing power acclaimed to be found in the ministry of Brother Coe. Coe, who in the 1950s was second in popularity only to Oral Roberts, had amassed a fortune estimated at one-half million dollars and now was attracting crowds numbering up to 6,000 to his revivals in this Miami campaign. The alleged healings, which were performed nightly, appeared to be many and miraculous in nature to the people who attended these revivals.[232,233]

The mother of the stricken child, Mrs. Ann Clark, stood in awe before this man, who had just finished the

163

laying on of hands on her son and, in compliance with his instructions, removed the braces from the boy's tiny, feeble legs. In anticipation she excitedly watched him try to take his first step; but the boy collapsed and fell to the floor. He was unable to walk. Believing that putting the braces back on her son's crippled feet would exhibit a lack of faith and prevent the still expected healing, she kept them off for two days after the revival. However, his legs began to swell, and in desperation she took him to a physician who, appalled at the actions that had been taken, ordered that the braces be placed back on immediately before any more possible irreparable harm would ensue. In the meantime the mother had also written a letter to Brother Coe asking for advice, but he ignored her pleas. Incensed, she then called the police and charged Coe with practicing medicine without license. Coe was jailed and released on $5,000 bail. During his trial Coe replied that while his faith in God is sufficient to cause healing, God is the healer. He [Coe] cannot heal anyone. All he does is simply practice his religion which happens to include faith healing. Scores of evangelists came to testify on his behalf. The court agreed with Coe, and the charges against him were dismissed. The Clarks then filed suit for damages against him, but before the case was settled Coe became critically ill. Coe had been outspoken against medical treatment, having stated that those who consulted physicians would have to take the "mark of the beast." Nevertheless, he did allow himself to be hospitalized. He died shortly thereafter of bulbar polio.[234,235,236]

Though this incident reportedly did not bring about a decline in the size of the crowds attending Coe's revivals, it did, nevertheless, provide nationwide adverse publicity for deliverance evangelism. It added fuel to the critics of the evangelists and led to widespread indignation against them.

The case of Clark versus Coe represents one of a series of incidents characterizing the turbulent relationship between deliverance evangelists and the greater society since this form of ministry came to public attention. These conflicts have involved notably the medical profession, governmental agencies, and organized religion. Of the various areas of the evangelists' activities that have come under repeated censure, it is their involvement in the healing of the believers that has promoted the greatest concern.

The Medical Profession Versus the Faith Healers

Through the years many faith healers have encountered opposition from physicians and public health officials. Around the turn of the century John Alexander Dowie, for example, was taken to court some 100 times in one year by the Chicago Board of Health.[237] Today the conflict is more subtle and in view of the findings in the area of psychosomatic medicine certain concessions have been made to faith healing. A publication of the American Medical Association was quoted to state:

> It cannot be denied that faith plays some part in over-coming illness. A sick person who thinks he is going to get well will do much better than one who gives up. It is only the spiritual quacks, those taking money from ill persons on promises of cures that are doubtful if not medically impossible, whom we vigorously oppose.[238]

Though it is recognized that faith healing may be a significant factor in curing certain patients, the conflict has continued to exist, and the opposition is far from appeased. Warnings are issued in statement after statement regarding the possible harmfulness of reliance on faith healing alone, even if the healer is not a quack or charlatan. Some of the more skeptical critics have flatly denied the possibility of the occurrence of miracles of healing, and their evaluation of the work of the faith healers is predominantly negative. According to one of them:

> I would not even recommend a terminal case—a patient who has been given up by all doctors—to go to a tent revival. Their record for healing is so poor that they can be dismissed from any serious consideration in the treating of the sick.

Lack of Proof as to the Effectiveness of the Faith Healer The attempts at scientific evaluation of the effectiveness of the deliverance evangelists have been meager. A follow-up study by a group of physicians, professors, lawyers, and ministers of the healing mission of Charles S. Price in Vancouver, B.C., found that of the 350 persons professed to have been healed, they could afterwards not detect any physical change in the symptoms or conditions of 301 cases, 39 died within six months following the healing mission, 5 became insane, and 5 others, suffering from various nervous disorders, apparently had been cured.[239]

William A. Nolen, a physician, who followed up numerous cases of alleged divine cures at Kathryn Kuhlman revivals, found no miraculous healings. According to him:

> Patients that go to a Kathryn Kuhlman service, paralyzed from the waist down as the result of injury to the spinal cord, never have been and never will be cured through the ministrations of Miss Kuhlman; Miss Kuhlman cannot cure a paralysis caused by a damaged spinal cord. The patient who suddenly discovers, at a Kuhlman service, that he can now move an arm or a leg that was previously paralyzed had that paralysis as a result of an emotional, not a physical, disturbance. Neurotics and hysterics will frequently be relieved of their symptoms by the suggestions and ministrations of charismatic healers. It is in treating patients of this sort that healers claim their most dramatic triumphs.[240]

A clinical psychologist, Louis Rose, has for many years investigated testimonies of people, to a large extent patients of the spiritualist Harry Edwards, who have claimed to have been cured by supernatural intervention. Rose concluded that while healings may occur which cannot be explained by our present state of knowledge, this does not mean that they are miracles. So far, in spite of the aid he has sought from the healers and the healed, he has not been able to uncover any evidence for the existence of paranormal cures, and the existence of even a single case of a miraculous healing has not yet been verified to his satisfaction.[241]

Admitting the possible effectiveness in treating ills of psychosomatic origin, the British Medical Association concluded that most of the supposed cures of organic disease through faith healing which they investigated could be explained by mistaken diagnosis, errors in prognosis, alleviation, remission, the effect of combined treatment, or spontaneous cure but found no indication that some divine power might be involved.[242]

Interference with Scientific Medical Treatment The critics at best admit that the deliverance evangelists can possibly deal with certain psychosomatic cases but that in the area of organic illnesses their ministration is ineffective or even outright harmful.

A frequent attack directed against faith healing, particularly as practiced by such healers as the deliverance evangelists, maintains that it interferes with the seeking of proper medical care and thus has grave potential for further impairment of the patient's health. The critics have maintained that the deliverance evangelists discourage patients from seeking prompt medical treatment in the early stages when illness can be most easily arrested, that they disseminate ideas inimical to the health of the believers, and that they mislead the sick into believing that they have been cured when they are not.

One incident where a mistaken belief that a cure had taken place led to tragic consequences in Barrie, Ont., in 1952. A 19-year-old girl, who had been suffering from diabetes since early childhood, attended the services of a R. W. Holmes, an itinerate evangelist. He prayed for her healing and told her to turn to God. Believed to possess sufficient faith to be cured, she stopped taking her insulin. Three days later she died as a consequence of this action.[243,244]

"A major problem is that people who need to be under a physician's care turn instead to faith healers, or they come to a physician after the faith healer has failed to cure their ills—by which time their disease might be far too advanced for even the best medical care to cope successfully with the patient's condition," stated a general practitioner who had a substantial number of patients from the lower socio-economic class, several of whom fluctuate between scientific medical treatment and various faith-healing systems.

The critics have pointed out not only that people are delayed or discouraged from seeking medical aid by faith healers, but also that at times they are given advice which is contradictory to that of the physicians.

At a tent meeting I attended in the early autumn of 1966 in Columbus, Ohio, the evangelist told his audience that those who are suffering from diabetes should stop taking their medications.

"If God can't heal you, nobody can . . . and if you have to take a shot all the time, you might as well be dead."

Then he pointed to one of his employees who supposedly had had so much faith in God that he stopped taking the insulin and now claimed to be completely cured.

During the same week in a storefront church in a different part of Columbus, another evangelist told an obese woman that God had just taken 20 pounds off of her instantaneously and that it was no longer necessary for her to continue the diet her doctor had prescribed, because God would take care of her.

By no means are all of the deliverance evangelists so dogmatically and blatantly outspoken against medical treatment. Nevertheless, the charge has been made that the underlying implications of their teaching often lead to unfavorable consequences.

The Problem of Temporary "Cures" After having George Jeffries pray for his healing in Liverpool, England, a man suffering from chronic encephalitis gave the following account of his experience:

> After inquiring the nature of my complaint, he laid his hands on my right temple and prayed fervently. I then felt what can be described as a current of healing power pass from him to me. As a result, I could walk a few steps without limping and the tremor ceased. He then asked was I cured, and, on receiving my reply in the affirmative, asked me to repeat "Thank you, Jesus." He then proclaimed my cure to the meeting. The effect, however, wore off. I estimate a period of about five minutes before the limp returned. The tremor, however, was absent and I remained free from it even at breakfast next morning. I was quite detached and had no emotional feelings beyond curiosity. I cannot explain the temporary cure.[245]

The critics have pointed out that temporary cures such as the one reported above can have serious side effects. The patients may begin to think they are cured when in effect they are not—their symptoms might have been eliminated but not the disease itself. As a result even the more skeptical persons may be lead to delay, if not completely stop, proper medical treatment. In addition, when the patients discover that, after all, they were not cured and may have actually harmed themselves, disillusionment or other psychological disturbances may at times follow as illustrated by an observer's report of a blind girl at one of Aimee McPherson's revival meetings:

> A little girl wore a pair of glasses one-half of which was entirely black. I gathered that she was totally blind in one eye and almost blind in the other. I sat upon the stage very close to the whole procedure. While prayer was being made for her, the little girl, who appeared to be about 11 years of age, wept and sobbed and writhed in her eagerness to secure the help that she had been led to expect. She left the platform and public claim was made by one of the workers that she had been healed, and the little girl verified the claim by a nod of the head given in reply to the question of the workers. An hour later, when the meeting was out, I noticed a small cluster of women near the platform. I thought I saw the blind little girl in their midst, so I asked my wife to go over and investigate and talk to her if necessary. She found the erstwhile "cured" girl flat on her face on the floor, sobbing, with shattered hopes and a breaking heart. Her disappointment was complete, and so was her disillusionment. The improved sight that she seemed to have had in the midst of the excitement on the platform had disappeared, and with it the hope of the little girl.[246]

The Governmental Agencies Versus the Faith Healers

Charges of Illegal Practice of Medicine   Since both the deliverance evangelists and physicians deal with the physical ills of the population, an overlap occurs between the functions they perform, with evangelists infringing on the realm which the physicians consider their prerogative. For that reason some of the critics of the faith healers raise the question whether they are not actually practicing medicine without license and are therefore subject to prosecution. This is the charge Mrs. Clark brought against Coe. Though the courts ruled in favor of Coe, the same accusation has been continued to be raised by other antagonists.

To deal with this problem, every state has enacted laws to regulate medical practice by specifying minimal standards that have to be met before the applicant can be duly licensed in his particular field. To diagnose, treat, or prescribe any form of medication for a disease or injury to a human being with the intention of receiving directly or indirectly any form of compensation, but without the license required in the community of the therapist's work, is a criminal offense, usually a misdemeanor. Likewise attaching any title or abbreviation which implies accreditation as a legitimate therapist without first being properly licensed for it is prohibited.[247]

All of these laws have attached clauses which exempt, in compliance to the guarantee of freedom of religion by our Constitution, from the licensing requirements persons who treat human ills solely by prayer or other spiritual means. Faith healers, such as the deliverance evangelists, who adhere exclusively to prayer or other spiritual means in dealing with the sick are perfectly within their legal rights to do so. They cannot be prosecuted for malpractice in regards to their attempts to heal because they are not hired to perform a medical function but instead are asked to pray. However, if the faith healer resorts to prescribing some substance such as holy water, or submit to any physical manipulation, then he can be prosecuted under the medical practice status in this country.[248]

Whenever challenged, the deliverance evangelists have been quick to point out that they do not heal—rather all healing comes from God. Repeatedly many of them have publicly declared their opposition to being labeled faith healers. By making these declarations the evangelists protect themselves from charges of practicing medicine without a license.[249]

Conflicts have become particularly bitter where medical care for minors has become an issue. The believers have charged that their religious beliefs have been undermined and their constitutional rights violated in cases such as the forcible removal of the Hart Children. (See Chapter 5.) The courts have disagreed. For more than 60 years they have consistently ruled that a parent who, even if prompted by sincere religious conviction, denies his child the medical care required by law, is guilty of a misdemeanor, and if the child dies, the parent may be charged with involuntary manslaughter. The parent-liability decisions have maintained that faith healers, along with other unorthodox therapists, do not constitute adequate medical care for a child. The parent who utilizes them in place of a qualified physician can be punished and the child taken into custody, by force if necessary, and provided with what society defines as adequate treatment. The parent may call both a qualified physician and a faith healer to treat the child but not solely a faith healer. The faith healer who strongly advises a parent to deny the medical aid required by law for his child can only be theoretically punished in this country as an accessory. There is no law to prevent the faith healer from urging the parents to rely on his method and to distrust the medical profession. Nor can a faith healer be prosecuted for malpractice if he undertakes to treat a sick child as long as he limits his involvement to prayer or other spiritual manipulations. An adult, however, is completely free to accept or reject medical aid and to follow the teachings of a faith healer no matter how preposterous the doctrines may be.[250]

In many cases of prosecution involving conflict between medical statutes and religious dogma, the decisions have clearly reflected the norm that where religion and medicine are practiced together, the constitutional right to freedom of religion does not justify the concurrent illegal practice of medicine.[251]

Charges of Fraud Governmental agencies have come in contact with deliverance evangelists also in cases involving charges of fraud. The critics have charged that fraud has been perpetrated sometimes by the healer, at other times by those who claim to be healed, at still other times through a conspiracy of both the healer and the patient. Even persons unfamiliar with this mode of religious practice are not unlikely to impute unsavory motives to these men and women. These beliefs have been further strengthened by the confessions of Marjoe Gortner and other exposés attempted by the mass media.

One reason for suspicions of fraud lies in the structure of deliverance evangelism. It has been proposed that faith healing is attractive to charlatans because it is outside of organized religion and is potentially a lucrative enterprise. Armstrong observed:

> All the major faith-healing cults, and most others, are organized as "religious bodies," although the majority are not affiliated with any organized denomination. Like churches, they are tax-exempt. They needn't report expenses or income, or disclose church-related business transactions. It was inevitable that unscrupulous persons would take advantage of this.[252]

Marjoe Gortner has supported this contention in his own case. Warner Brothers had offered $10,000 a week to make a child actor out of him. This offer was turned down by his parents because, according to Marjoe, the money would have been put in trust and an accounting of it would have to be made of it. Instead, it was decided to keep him preaching where the money was all in cash, untaxed, and not accountable to anyone.[253]

High pressure or irregular methods of obtaining finances, the affluent life-style, and phony healings have been cited by the critics as reasons why they feel the deliverance evangelists are charlatans. Stegall has

173

argued that these evangelists are not simple and sincere, but deluded men trying to propagate the Gospel and relieve the suffering of the sick and disabled. Rather, they are seeking personal prestige and financial gain. They are, according to Stegall, quacks who cannot deliver what they claim to be able to produce—for why else would they be so afraid of any kind of an investigation?[254]

Not all, of course, have been afraid of investigations. Kathryn Kuhlman, for one, was reportedly very cooperative with attempts to verify cures attributed to her ministry. From my own experience, I found Don Stewart quite willing to talk to me. He appeared not to be bothered by any of the questions or criticisms I directed at him. Several others have likewise been receptive to giving interviews. But I also encountered evangelists that were suspiciously evasive. They or their aides went to considerable lengths, including lying, to avoid me. All this left the impression that they might have something to hide. Many reporters have attested to the difficulties of getting answers to even a few simple queries. In his article in *Reader's Digest,* Armstrong stated:

> The most damaging evidence against commercialized faith healers is their firm refusal to submit their alleged miracles of healing to medical examination. I sent letters making such a request to about a dozen of the better-known healers. Only one replied. He declared that his results "needed no further proof, for those who have faith."[255]

Another reason why critics have come to feel that fraud is involved is that the claims of the evangelists regarding instantaneous healings and other miracles not only differ from their own religious convictions but often go beyond their belief. Not able to accept the reality of these claims, the critics have offered alternative explanations for what appears to be occurring at the old-time revivals. They have charged that these "healings" are faked and that the supposedly afflicted individuals are simply hired to present falsified testimony. Furthermore, the critics have attested, the "healings" that are not faked have been previously handpicked to assure as much as possible that they can be easily manipulated and presented as a dramatic spectacle to the onlookers.

Reports of incidents have been circulated which seem to give at least some credence to these charges. A Foursquare missionary in the Congo, who filed a suit against Aimee McPherson, revealed that Sister Aimee sometimes had in her healing line a woman with a slow-leaking balloon concealed under her dress. With a pin, Sister Aimee would puncture the balloon, miraculously curing the "goiter."[256] Another person who had also been an active member of the revival scene wrote that regularly among those supposedly miraculously cured by one evangelist during the 1960s was his tent manager, who would jump from the stretcher and dramatically run around the congregation.[257]

Stegall concluded that these kinds of misrepresentations probably do not occur frequently, since they constitute an unnecessary risk for healers, who can get "enough neurotics and dupes to support their publicity programs without fraud."[258]

Evidence has indicated that at least some fraudulent or unintentionally misleading testimony is given by people claiming cures. People have claimed to have experienced miraculous cures at revival meetings—yet upon follow-up their ailments have been found to persist. It has been postulated that the healers, perhaps unconsciously, have edited their patients' testimonies and have suggested appropriate responses to them.[259] In other cases it might be the patients' desire for recognition or simply wishful thinking that led to exaggerated claims.

Nolen's investigation of Kathryn Kuhlman's revivals led him to believe that while she was neither a liar nor a charlatan, many misleading testimonies were presented by people claiming to have received a miraculous healing. Nolen explained the reason for this as having been due largely to the structure of the revival meeting. There, according to him, it became almost more difficult *not* to claim a cure than to claim one. A major reason for all this apparently was that the people who testified did not want to let Kathryn Kuhlman down. Others desperately wanted to believe. Furthermore, the atmosphere created by the charisma of the evangelist, the music and hymns, and the multitudes of testimonies to healings can be conducive to produce illusions among the sick and handicapped that their problems have suddenly vanished. Nolen stated that the mood at Kuhlman's revivals became almost impossible to resist:

"You wanted to believe so badly you could hardly stand it. You didn't want to reason; you wanted to accept."[260]

Nolen was speaking from personal experiences. He and a friend of his had come to the revival meeting as skeptical observers. His friend, who suffered from a heart condition, stated that he experienced a sensation every time Kuhlman mentioned that someone was being cured of this ailment. Several times he was ready to stand up and claim a cure. But each time someone else beat him to it by claiming it first. Nolen had a similar experience. Whenever she said someone was being cured of bursitis, he found himself testing his elbow. The next day, to their disappointment, they found their conditions were unchanged.[261]

Court Convictions   While charges of fraud against deliverance evangelists and other faith healers have been frequent and intense, convictions in court have been rare. A major issue involved here is that many people are unaware of the courts' interpretation of the Constitutional guarantee of religious freedom. What to many is fraud and misrepresentation, such as Father Divine's obviously fraudulent claim to be God Himself, is to the courts simply his right to exercise his "religious convictions." No matter how contradictory to all the facts we possess or absurd the claims of the faith healer (or the other religious leaders), the truth or falsity of this "religious doctrine" cannot be tried by a jury nor can he be prosecuted for the crime of obtaining money under false pretenses if he appears to be more or less sincere. But if he does not believe in the religious doctrines he promulgated and deliberately uses them to deceive people for financial gains, he then can be convicted of fraud if specified proof can be obtained.[262] Telling lies that are not directly connected with soliciting funds and conjuring tricks that are presented as supernatural wonders appear to be quite legal, since deeds of this kind have been proven against some of the evangelists but no legal action against them was taken.

More often specific confrontations with the law enforcement agencies have centered on relatively minor issues. The evangelists have been brought to court on the charge of disturbing the peace because of the highly emotional nature of the revival meeting, or they have been found to be guilty of failure to comply with certain municipal codes involving permits or other technical matters.

Occasionally, however, the evangelists have been charged and convicted of more serious breaches of the law. There have been cases of drunken driving and other misconduct. Bud Chambers was convicted in 1976 of conspiring to transport eight stolen cars and trucks across state lines. Although the evangelist and his wife drove several of the cars for personal use, they were primarily used for business in connection with Chambers' Glorious Church, Inc., particularly in connection with the tent revivals. Chambers denied in court any knowledge that the vehicles were stolen. But the jury decided to believe the key witness against Chambers, a boxer turned part-time preacher, who testified that he had sold the vehicles to Chambers at a very low price and informed him on several occasions that they were stolen.[263] The judge fined Chambers $2,000 and placed him on five-years probation.[264]

One successful conviction for fraud involved a national radio evangelist, Rev. J. Charles Jessup. He was found guilty in 1968 of using the mails to defraud. The indictment against him stated that over the previous 20 years his faith-healing activities had netted over $10 million on promise to finance religious and missionary activities, but instead he used the money to buy a house, expensive cars, boats, and a seaplane. The specific charge on which he was tried involved a broadcast in 1961, during which he announced that he would have to go off the air unless he received some contributions during that week. Yet all along he knew that the radio station had been paid in advance for the next three years. Pleading "no contest," Jessup was fined the maximum of $2,000 and sentenced to one year in prison and five-years' probation. In pronouncing the sentence, the judge reportedly admonished him:

"For all these years you have been pretending to pray *for* people, and you have been preying *on* them."[265]

Organized Religion Versus the Faith Healers

From the earliest beginnings of deliverance evangelism in this country conflict has centered on its religious doctrine. Opposition from the clergy to their calling has been reported by such 19th-century evangelists as G. O. Barnes and Willis Brown as well as by Oral Roberts and A. A. Allen. Allen noted that continued opposition to his ministry has come from preachers. His many predicaments have included being expelled from the Assemblies of God Church and being publicly condemned by a spokesman of the Sacramento Council of Churches.[266] One of the most formidable critics of Oral Roberts and other healing evangelists was the

Presbyterian minister, Rev. Carroll R. Stegall. Congregations of the Churches of Christ used to place ads in the newspapers attacking Roberts' ministry. Believing that no man has the power for divine healing, they have offered a $1,000 reward for proof of just one miraculous cure occurring at the old-time revival meeting.

It has been noted that many of the churches who had opposed the practices of the deliverance evangelists in the 1960s were a decade later much more tolerant, even supportive, of these same practices and strengthened their hold on the Neo-Pentecostals among their own members. Although much of the conflict between organized religion and the evangelists appeared to have subsided, some of the evangelical churches in the mid-1970s stepped up their campaign against the healing evangelists, labeling them as charlatans. Other churches were urging the Neo-Pentecostals within their congregations to repudiate the more extreme claims of the evangelists.[267] Concerns have been expressed by several clergymen I interviewed regarding the evangelists' interpretations of the Bible and the consequences of their doctrines for the believers.

The Issue of Faith Healing   The issue of faith healing alone has raised many controversies and theological debates, with some of the critics stating that it is not in accordance with the Bible, that no supernatural forces impinge on the healing process, and that psychic damage can easily result as a consequence of this practice. Even those of a relatively fundamentalistic persuasion have acknowledged that while miracles of healing did take place during the early days of Christianity, they no longer occur in the contemporary world. The Jehovah's Witnesses are outspokenly opposed to contemporary faith healers and Roman Catholic shrines. They believe that although Jesus did perform miraculous cures and passed on the power to heal to his disciples, they were the last ones to possess it. The Jehovah's Witnesses do accept institutionalized medical care with one important reservation—they refuse to submit to a blood transfusion because of the Biblical commandment not to eat blood.[268]

The Commission on Theology and Church Relations of The Lutheran Church—Missouri Synod stated:

> . . . we should recognize that this gift of the Spirit does not necessarily include the promise of all extraordinary spiritual gifts that were once given to the apostolic church, such as speaking in tongues, miracles of healing or prophecy. According to the pattern of Sacred Scripture, God does not necessarily give His church in all ages the same special gifts. . . . even in the apostolic church, where the gifts of tongues and healing were very evident, it is not clear that all Christians possessed these charismatic gifts. . . . The Christian church must therefore be extremely careful not to place too much emphasis on any one of these gifts. . . . In the light of recent developments in Christendom, the Lutheran Church is also deeply concerned lest the functions of the Spirit be emphasized in a manner that would tend to make the saving work of Christ appear less important.[269]

In 1962 a committee of physicians, ministers, and theologians was appointed by The United Lutheran Church in America to study the faith healers. The committee concluded that the faith healers tend to be less concerned with the spiritual and physical well-being of the people than with the demonstration of their personal power or the attainment of fame and financial gain. Healers were charged with making a spectacle of human misery and exploiting the hopes and fears of the desperate, the disturbed, and the credulous.[270]

The antagonism is not limited to specific historic churches which are critical of or not involved to any extent with faith healing but can also be found among ministers who themselves are convinced of the efficacy of faith healing. One Protestant minister, himself active in promoting the practice of praying for the sick, saw a distinct, qualitative difference between the healing ministry of the deliverance evangelists and that found within organized religion, the latter being in his opinion vastly superior to the former:

"Christ was a faith healer. In the history of the church there are many instances where people have claimed to be healed by faith. . . . The healing a minister does would come under the category of faith healing. But it is not a part of the main emphasis in the main churches. We pray for people who are sick that they be healed. We anoint them with oil as it says in the Bible. . . ."

He found very significant differences between the healings practiced by a minister and those of the healing evangelists:

"The people seek the ministers out; they ask you, you don't ask them. Ministers do not claim to have any great unusual power, where as many of the faith healers do. Faith healing, in that sense, is religious quackery. The faith healer is not tied to anyone or anything; he has no responsibility to the people."[271]

He expressed concern that the high pressure tactics used by the evangelists lead the poor to contribute sums of money beyond their means and that the emotion-laden atmosphere of the revivals promotes a false sense of well-being and divine intervention in healing.

This minister and others who have been in sympathy with the practice of faith healing have come to regard the mass healing meetings as a danger to the spiritual and psychological condition of the believers.[272,273] The committee of The United Lutheran Church in America charged that faith healers endanger the spiritual life of the believers by leaving the implication that failure to be cured is due to lack of faith on the part of the afflicted.[274] Even followers of those deliverance evangelists who do not blame failure on lack of faith

181

may, nevertheless, come to hold this view. Kathryn Kuhlman repeatedly stated that she did not even know what faith is, that some who have it are not healed while some who do not have it are healed. Yet, Nolen found that among those who did not receive a cure, none blamed Kathryn Kuhlman, most blamed themselves, feeling that somehow they were at fault or perhaps they were not spiritually ready to be cured. He perceived much disappointment on the part of those who were not healed.[275] Critics have commented that disillusionment that follows failure to receive a cure or temporary cures cause a loss of faith in general. They have claimed that the believers thought that they had a positive relationship with God but as they see that their condition becomes only worse they interpret this to mean that God has deserted them, and the grief that they are likely to experience then must be profound.[276, 277]

Opposition from Other Pentecostals

Even Pentecostals, both lay and clergy, have entered into this conflict. While some Pentecostal and Holiness groups have given whole-hearted support to the contemporary deliverance evangelists, others have had strong reservations in regard to them or have gone so far as to unequivocally reject them.

When the salvation-healing campaigns came into prominence in the late 1940s, they were initially accepted enthusiastically within the Pentecostal movement. Soon, however, according to Brumback, this ministry began to be exploited by men with selfish aims:

A number of the men and women to whom God has given an exceptional healing ministry merit the highest respect; and their ministry will survive the closest scrutiny. They have been used of God to revitalize the faith of thousands of Pentecostal preachers and laymen [by] healing. . . . By means of radio, television, periodicals and huge campaigns these salvation-healing evangelists have been able to carry the full gospel to millions at home and abroad. Nevertheless, it became manifest, after a short time, that nature had mixed with grace. Some evangelists, by their unscriptural and unethical actions, began to bring disrepute upon the whole healing ministry. Their supreme egotism, their arrogant attitude toward all who dared to counsel with them, their claims of healings which were not verified, their disparagement of the "feeble efforts" of the ministers and missionaries . . . their lack of self-denial and, at times, their outright racketeering caused many pastors and congregations to suffer a severe "backwash" of public opinion.[278]

Many Pentecostals started to complain that the deliverance evangelists featured healing of the body more than salvation of the soul, and that their "prosperity" teaching emphasized that material gain is an unmistakable sign of godliness.[279]

Don Stewart, during a campaign in California a number of years ago that he held jointly with Dale Davis, another Pentecostal preacher, found himself involved in one aspect of this conflict:

In the first few days of the meeting, our crowds were under fifty at each service. One reason was that the promised support of some twenty local Pentecostal ministers didn't materialize. Dale had gone to considerable trouble in urging them to sponsor and participate in the meeting. But an independent, interdenominational ministry without ties to any one church runs into roadblocks. Instead of fellowship under God, there often is jealousy and pettiness. Sadly, the area ministers frequently resent a "hotshot" evangelist who moves in and out because they are fearful offerings and sheep from their flocks will be "stolen." And in my case there was disapproval of my public demonstrations of healing. Though public healing is of the Bible—Jesus performed His miracles before crowds or a goodly number of witnesses—not all Pentecostal churches, to say nothing of other denominations, practice or approve of public healing.[280]

At least some fraudulent practices exist among the deliverance evangelists that have negative consequences on the spiritual life of the believers. This is reluctantly admitted by even some of those with a vested interest, the most ardent supporters of this ministry. Gordon Lindsay stated that the majority of the evangelists are true men of God but, just as in the early Bible days, a few are not. The tragedy of this is that far too often a believer blindly follows disreputable leaders until finally he comes to realize that he has been duped. The consequences, according to Lindsay, are that the believer becomes disillusioned and backslides. Lindsay cautioned that believers must look out for warning signs such as magical claims connected with prayer cloths, promises of wealth to those who contribute, and sensational publicity stunts.[281]

A particularly devastating attack came from G. H. Montgomery, a believer in and supporter of deliverance evangelism. Montgomery had been a close adviser to Oral Roberts and editor of his magazine. In 1961 the two quarreled bitterly and Montgomery threatened to release to the press a file that would discredit Roberts. In the series of articles published in Juanita Coe's *International Healing Magazine,* he attacked, without naming names, the character and motives of many deliverance evangelists. He denounced the false and exaggerated claims made by them, their fake gimmicks, phony healings, selfishness, and preoccupation with money and material comforts. He maintained that some of them were nothing but drunkards and degenerates. He revealed that one successful evangelist had a drinking and drug problem, was blackmailed by an inmate of a penitentiary, committed adultery, and mistreated his wife; that one evangelist who came to Jamaica reported about twice as many converts there as the entire population of that country; and that of nearly $1 million raised for a specific project of one evangelist, the inventory showed that less than 5 percent had actually been used for the work for which the people had donated this money.[282]

Montgomery blamed not only the character of the evangelists for these abuses but also the alleged jealousy and short-sightedness of the Pentecostal denominations. He felt that instead of supervising and controlling the evangelists, the churches actually had forced the evangelists to extremes and sometimes even searched for means to excommunicate them. Thus, there emerged independent evangelistic associations that were not accountable to anyone.[283]

In Defense of the Evangelists

When Jack Coe came to trial in Miami over the Clark incident, he was not short of supporters. One of many to testify on his behalf was Gordon Lindsay. As to the failure of Mrs. Clark's polio-stricken son to receive a healing, Lindsay stated:

Actually this woman knew nothing about the conditions upon which Divine healing is based. She had heard that miracles were taking place in the tent, and she had only one thought, and that was to get her child in the healing line. When she was told to wait her turn, and to receive instruction for healing, she became hysterical, soundly abusing the workers for not letting her get her boy into the healing line at once. She was to later testify on the witness stand that she belonged to a nominal church but had not attended for eight years. Because she made herself such a nuisance in trying to get her child prayed for, the workers permitted her on the second night to get

185

her child in the line. There were hundreds to be ministered to that night, and Brother Coe, when he came to the woman told her . . . "If you believe Jesus heals the child, take the braces off, and leave them off." This was an act of faith, commonly called for even by Jesus when He ministered to the sick. But no minister of Divine healing makes a guarantee that people who are not serving God, will be healed, neither they nor their children.[284]

The evangelists and their supporters have perceived this and other attacks on their ministry as persecution by those who are hostile to or lack an understanding of their particular religious convictions. They have pointed out how easy it is to make all kinds of accusations and subtle innuendos that will bring discredit to even the most innocent victim. Yet refuting these charges with the kind of proof demanded may remain a virtually impossible task and unfeasible as to the amount of time and effort it might consume. For these reasons they say that they have simply ignored the attacks perpetrated against them. Jack Coe stated that it would be a waste of his time, which would be better spent in doing God's work. W. V. Grant admitted the difficulty of obtaining the kind of proof that would satisfy the critics, in reference to such phenomena as the occurrence of divine cures:

"Medical doctors are businessmen. . . . They are not in the habit of signing their name to statements and getting tangled up in religious quarrels. . . . They will not swear that they *know* God healed him. This the fighters of God's power know."[285]

The Reality of Faith Healing The evangelists have readily admitted the charges that multitudes of truly suffering individuals fail to be healed of their ailments and leave the revival meeting in the same physical condition in which they arrived. At the height of his healing ministry Oral Roberts stated that he would be the happiest man in the world if he could bring health to 25 percent of those who asked for it.[286]

Their attempts to explain the failures has varied. Some place the blame on the lack of faith in the patient. Others, in contrast, maintained that even atheists can be cured and proceed to bring forth many cases to that effect. Jack Coe conceded that many he prayed for were not healed, adding:

> I began asking God to show me why they were not healed. I had prayed with as much faith for them as for those who were healed! God revealed to me that many did not understand how to receive healing. They needed instruction in His word concerning His will and power. I firmly believe that more people would be healed if they only knew how to accept and keep it![287]

Several have admitted that they simply do not know why some are healed and others are not.

All this, evangelists maintain, does not mean that divine cures do not occur and is no reason for undermining the healing ministry. Vic Coburn has felt that he and his colleagues have been treated very unfairly in this respect. He pointed out that if a faith healer prays for a patient and the patient does not receive a cure, the faith healer is censured and is accused of taking advantage of the ill and getting up their hopes falsely. If the patient dies there is adverse publicity all across the nation. But what about all the people who go to physicians and are not healed? Coburn stated that in the files of physicians are records of many cases of patients they treated who later died and of patients who died after they pronounced them cured. Many people who come to him have been given up by physicians and have spent all of their life savings on medical care. Coburn is their last hope. He argues that the faith-healing ministry should receive the same benefits of doubt as medical science. Physicians, according to him, merely assist the natural recovery process which God instilled in men, while he in his ministry invokes God's healing power to bring forth instantaneous, miraculous cures.[288] That miracles of healing actually do take place is proclaimed with utmost assurance by all the evangelists.

"Miracles—miraculous healings—are Christ's way of telling us to prepare for Him. There are more miraculous healings now, in the 1970s, than there have been at any other time since the days of the early Church," observed Kathryn Kuhlman.[289]

And there is no lack of corroboration for this by people who claim to have been recipients of these miracles. I was able to follow up one such person, a retired high school principal who attended a revival held by Evangelist W. V. Grant. For over two years he had painful sores on his feet that had not responded to medical treatment. On the recommendation of some of his acquaintances he agreed to go to one of Grant's healing campaigns. He did not believe that he would be helped, but what did he have to lose by going?

At the revival meeting Grant picked him out of the congregation and told him things about himself that astounded him since supposedly only he and his wife knew about them. Then Grant prayed for his healing, having diagnosed his illness only in the vaguest terms. Immediately afterwards the sores on his feet began to improve and within a week or two were completely healed.

This man was a well-educated person, liked and respected by his neighbors and acquaintances. He was considered honest and dependable. Many had known of his difficulties with the sores on his feet, and they were able to verify that he was completely cured after the revival.

A coincidence, or the workings of psychosomatic factors? To the former school principal it was a miracle. It deeply affected his religious convictions and convinced him that W. V. Grant was truly a man of God.

The evangelists are also able to produce cases which appear to go beyond the psychosomatic and have even baffled the experts. The following is one of several such cases reported by *Time* magazine as having occurred at Kathryn Kuhlman revivals:

> Paul Garnreiter, the seven-year old boy who regained his hearing . . . had suffered a proteus infection in his left ear for four years. A mastoidectomy two years ago showed a severely deteriorated eardrum. Last week Paul's physician could find no evidence of damage.[290]

Psychic researcher, Allen Spraggett, who has not been impressed by many of the prominent deliverance evangelists, has, nevertheless, concluded that at least Kathryn Kuhlman was a saint. Contrary to the findings of Dr. Nolen, Spraggett became convinced that Kuhlman was psychically gifted and that true miracles of healing have occurred through her ministry. He also felt that evidence supports the contention that prayer releases a force that stimulates healing.[291]

Dr. H. Richard Casdorph, a physician who possesses impressive scientific credentials, likewise set out to investigate alleged miraculous cures. His investigation was supplemented by a panel of noted physicians who evaluated those aspects of cases that fell within their field of specialization. Casdorph concluded that miraculous cures occur. Among others, he documented the instantaneous cure at a Kathryn Kuhlman revival of a woman who had been suffering from multiple sclerosis.[292]

Casdorph believes that Jesus healed the sick and raised the dead and that these miracles still occur today. Though he acknowledged that modern medicine has achieved miracles of its own, he justifies the practice of faith healers who at times urge patients to rely on God alone. He recorded Kathryn Kuhlman as having proclaimed at the conclusion of one of her revivals:

> Someone has been healed of a spinal condition but has not claimed the healing and come forward. If this individual does not do so and leaves this auditorium without claiming his healing, he will lose it.[293]

This, he feels, explains why some people are not healed. Casdorph is in agreement with many deliverance evangelists when he states:

> Whatever the reason, there are times when an answer to prayer is dependent on our trustful obedience, whether it be to remove a brace, to stand in a service, to go to a meeting, or to come home from a hospital. . . . Sometimes we must abandon medical treatments. Whatever, the key is trusting obedience to God's true guidance.[294]

Regarding persistent charges of lack of sufficient evidence of the existence of miracles and the failure of many deliverance evangelists to cooperate with investigators, the proponents have countered that they have all the proof they need as to the efficacy of faith healing: they have statements from the Bible about the reality of miracles, they have seen public displays of miracles, and there are far too many testimonies for them to be faked. Those who have failed to receive a physical cure might still have received a spiritual miracle, and their suffering has been made more bearable.

The proponents have further pointed out to the critics that the super-natural does not lend itself readily to scientific verification. Vivian Tenny, a physician-turned-faith-healer, claimed that when one is being used by God for spiritual healing the channel must be kept clear for the healing to flow through. She insisted that recording miracles blocks the free flow of the healing power.[295] Some of the deliverance evangelists have made similar statements, maintaining that the very presence of unbelievers hinders the ability of the sick to receive healing.

Several others have been quoted to say that "God does not submit to test-tube experiments." A Methodist mentioned that "the presence of an investigator breathing down one's neck . . . would destroy that un-self-consciousness so essential in true spiritual healing." Frederick Knowles, a Canadian who practiced faith healing before he became a physician, claims to have demonstrated that the paranormal gifts which he believed he possessed did actually vanish under laboratory conditions.[296] One investigator has concluded that in general all who claim psychic powers became inhibited when subjugated to rigid verification procedure, so that their alleged capabilities can be rarely experienced or produced under experimental conditions.[297]

The Ethics of the Profession The deliverance evangelists have complained that their ranks have included charlatans, adulterers, and drunkards, and that cases of misappropriation of funds have not been uncommon.[298] This, however, is not to be construed as a blanket indictment of the entire profession. There is no profession, including the ministry and medicine, that has managed to remain free of unscrupulous individuals. The evangelists have repeatedly insisted that there is no evidence that they as a whole are less ethical than other ministers.[299] Vic Coburn stated that there have been many abuses within the practice of medicine—incompetence, negligence, and unnecessary surgeries. Still the doctors are idolized and placed on an abnormally high pedestal.[300] But if just one of them commits a questionable act, the evangelists have argued, the entire profession is attacked. Many of the prominent evangelists were reportedly angered by Marjoe Gortner's exposé. They considered him an obscure figure in the movement who presented a distorted view of the profession.[301]

For the most part, evangelists have proclaimed, they are sincere and dedicated men and women whose calling has received a divine blessing. Testimonies to the saintly character of these evangelists abound. As to charges of preoccupation with financial profits, they have replied that it costs a great deal of money to do God's work. Besides, they have claimed that wealth is actually a sign of God's blessing.

The evangelists have consistently emphasized that all of their beliefs and practices, including this prosperity gospel, have Scriptural support and represent the true interpretation of the Bible. They feel that their best defense is the Bible itself, and they quote freely from it to justify their interpretation of it.

"The healings . . . and everything we believe in is based on the Bible. . . . These things are not something we make up out of air," concluded one evangelist.

"I preach healing," stated Don Stewart, and pointed out the Scriptural justification for it. " 'Behold, I cast out devils, and I do cures today and tomorrow'—Luke 13:32. Jesus Christ Himself took our sicknesses and carried away our diseases. Christ regarded this practical work of healing as an integral part of His ministry and includes it in His charge to His disciples down to the present day. 'And they went forth, and preached everywhere, the Lord working with them, and confirming the word with signs following.' "[302]

In the opinion of one Pentecostal historian, David E. Harrell, himself of a different religious persuasion, the successful deliverance evangelists possess a charismatic personality and administrative abilities. They have been exceptionally innovative and imaginative and have been willing to gamble their careers on a new venture. They are gifted, adventurous, rugged individualists. Some, such as Jack Coe, have been recklessly bold. For Oral

Roberts a great asset in his career has been his basic honesty.[303]

Their work has placed enormous pressures on them. Harrell has described them as burdened by work, adored by their followers, tempted by large sums of money, and so they end up as "trapped men." By becoming the "victims of hero worshipers who demand super-father figures, the evangelists frequently found little outlet for their human needs and weaknesses."[304]

Furthermore, Harrell maintains, a one-sided, negative view has prevailed in the mass media, and they have not received the proper recognition they deserve. The American public has been unable to distinguish between the moderate and the radical evangelists and are suspicious of even the most responsible evangelists.[305] Thus, the stereotype of them as charlatans has become pervasive.

According to Harrell, there are con men and racketeers among the evangelists, but most of them are neither saints nor charlatans. Though highly talented, they are pretty much like the ordinary sinners and share the faith and hopes of their followers.[306] The following rationalization was given for the misconduct of a controversial evangelist:

> One evangelist widely branded a hypocrite was . . . a psychologically crippled man who found it impossible to live with his public image. His lapses into alcoholism and dissipation were as abhorrent to him as to others, but his turbulent personality drove him from the peaks of glory to the depths of sin.[307]

Chapter 9

In Conclusion

Many different types of faith healers have established practices in this country. The ones most familiar to the general public are the deliverance evangelists. These men and women have combined "that old-time religion" with spectacular public healings in their revival crusades. The alleged miraculous cures taking place in their ministry have brought international acclaim to some of them. Scores of others, however, have remained small time practitioners, obscured from public notice.

The individuals who enter this calling tend to come from the rural areas and small towns of the southern part of the country. Many of them experienced economically hard times during their youth and, lacking an interest in formal education, decided to drop out of school.

Having established themselves on the gospel circuit, these evangelists generally proved themselves to be enterprising organizers and talented performers. They have been able to find many rewards from their calling, yet enormous pressures have been connected with it also. There are insecurities and fierce competition. Family life might be disrupted. Not just a few of them have curtailed their activities because of failing health or inability to cope with the psychological demands.

Throughout this century the popularity of the deliverance evangelists has fluctuated widely. By the mid-

1970s they continued to attract many followers who, according to one estimate, were donating $30-50 million a year to the various independent evangelistic associations.[308] Their followers have attested that the revival crusades have provided a meaningful form of religious worship from them and a means of dealing with their problems. Testimonies abound as to the saintly character of the evangelists.

The deliverance evangelists have attracted not only devoted followers but also hostile critics. Many of these critics have charged that they are charlatans who are taking advantage of the troubled and the gullible for their own private gain. Even the evangelists themselves and other proponents of this form of ministry have expressed serious concern about the motives and tactics of a segment of this profession. As to how prevalent the existence of frauds is among them, no one has been able to determine. It may well be concluded, however, that much more than just an occasional unscrupulous individual has infiltrated their ranks.

The evangelists have faced rejection, ridicule, and charges of fraud because in many ways they have violated society's expectations of a man of God. Many of them have become noted for their flamboyance, affluent life-style, exaggerations, and high-pressure techniques in soliciting contributions. Also the form of religious worship and doctrines they promote is different from what many Americans find acceptable and credible. More than anything else it has been their direct involvement with physical ailments that has brought down the greatest amount of censure on their ministry.

It has been conceded that the evangelists might have successes in dealing with such functional illnesses and personality disorders as drug addiction and alcoholism. As to clear-cut organic ailments, a true believer may well be aided in coming to terms with his condition, as well as possibly be aided in the healing process, since a relationship between emotional states and physical processes has been demonstrated. But there have also been harmful consequences when doctrines contrary to the advice of the physicians have been promoted, when the patient has neglected to use proper medical facilities, and when in a moment of emotionalism the patient has become convinced in his own mind that a miraculous cure has taken place and he acts upon it by refusing insulin or by removing an essential brace prematurely.

But is it possible that at least occasionally miracles of healing do occur? The findings of studies have been generally inconclusive. Many have rejected the possibility, while others, including a number of physicians, have come to believe in them. Certainly cures have been recorded that have baffled the experts. Even skeptics have been converted by what to them was proof of miraculous healings.

Over the years, while conducting my investigation of deliverance evangelism, I met many individuals who testified that they had received a miraculous cure, and I witnessed many claims to instantaneous cures at the revival meetings. But I was not able to obtain enough proof for any of them to convince me that they were true miracles of healing. At no time did I encounter anyone who even testified to something like the regrowth of a severed arm or leg. Nor am I, according to some of the devotees of faith healing, likely ever to witness it, because, they claim, to see a severed limb instantaneously restored would destroy faith by pushing it into the realm of certainty:

> . . . it is decidedly unlikely that a limb would be regrown . . . because to use His power this way would be to take from man his means of salvation—faith—based on our free will to believe or reject the Lord.[309]

Table I

Region and Division of Birth of the Deliverance Evangelists

Region	Division	Number	%
North East		2	4
	New England	0	
	Middle Atlantic	2	
North Central		10	19
	East North Central	4	
	West North Central	6	
South		33[a]	63
	South Atlantic	6	
	East South Central	5	
	West South Central	21	
West		6	12
	Mountain	2	
	Pacific	4	
Outside the U.S.A.		1	2
Total		52	100

[a] For one evangelist only region was reported.

Table II

Type of Area of Birth of the Deliverance Evangelists

Type of Area	Number	%
Farm	20	53
Village or small town	13	34
Medium or large city (100,000 or more)	5	13
Total	38	100

Table III

Socio-Economic Class of the Deliverance Evangelists' Family of Orientation

Socio-Economic Class	Number	%
Lower	24	71
Working and lower middle	10	29
Upper middle and upper	0	0
Total	34	100

Table IV

The Occupation of the Father of the Deliverance Evangelists

Occupation	Number	%
Farmer	15	44
Evangelist, preacher, or missionary (including farmer-preacher)	12	35
Unskilled and semi-skilled labor	5	15
Small businessman	2	6
Total	34	100

Table V

Religious Affiliation of the Parents of the Deliverance Evangelists

Religious Affiliation	Number	%
Protestant	45	83
Roman Catholic	4	7
Jewish	3	6
No religion	2	4
Total	54	100

Table VI

Stability of the Family of Orientation of the Deliverance Evangelists

Stability of Parents' Marriage	Number	%
Broken	16	32
Unbroken	34	68
Total	50	100

Bibliography and Notes

1. "Insulin Disregarded; Son to 'Live Again'," *The South Bend Tribune*, Aug. 27, 1973.
2. Ibid.
3. "The Exorcist," *Newsweek*, Sept. 10, 1973.
4. "Insulin Disregarded; Son to 'Live Again'," *The South Bend Tribune*, Aug. 27, 1973.
5. James Morris, *The Preachers* (New York: St. Martin's Press, 1973).
6. David Edwin Harrell Jr., *All Things Are Possible* (Bloomington, Ind.: Indiana University Press, 1975).
7. J. Morris, op. cit.
8. Oral Roberts, *My Story* (Tulsa: Summit Book Co., 1961).
9. Oral Roberts, *My Twenty Years of a Miracle Ministry* (Tulsa: [n. pub.], 1967).
10. Oral Roberts, *The Call* (New York: Doubleday, 1972).
11. O. Roberts, *My Twenty Years of a Miracle Ministry*, p. 7.
12. Ibid.
13. Evelyn Roberts, *I Married Oral Roberts* (Bixby, Okla.: Summit Book Co., 1956).
14. O. Roberts, *My Story*.
15. O. Roberts, *My Twenty Years of a Miracle Ministry*.
16. Ibid., p. 9.
17. Will Oursler, *The Healing Power of Faith* (New York: Hawthorn Books, Inc., 1957)
18. O. Roberts, *My Story*.

19. D. E. Harrell Jr., op. cit.
20. O. Roberts, *My Twenty Years of a Miracle Ministry*.
21. Allen Spragett, *Kathryn Kuhlman: The Woman Who Believes in Miracles* (New York: The World Publishing Co., 1970).
22. Aimee Semple McPherson, *The Story of My Life* (Hollywood: An International Correspondents' Pub., 1951).
23. Frank S. Mead, *Handbook of Denominations in the United States* (Nashville: Abingdon Press, 1965).
24. D. E. Harrell Jr., op. cit., p. 9
25. D. E. Harrell Jr., op. cit.
26. Ibid.
27. Ibid.
28. O. Roberts, *My Twenty Years of a Miracle Ministry*, p. 8.
29. William Thompson Price, *Without Scrip or Purse* (Louisville, Ky.: W. T. Price, 1883), p. 285.
30. W. T. Price, op. cit.
31. W. T. Price, op. cit., pp. 332–333.
32. W. T. Price, op. cit.
33. Ralph H. Major, *Faiths That Healed* (New York: D. Appleton-Century Co., 1940).
34. Harold Mehling, *The Scandalous Scamps* (New York: Henry Holt and Co., 1956).
35. R. H. Major, op. cit.
36. H. Mehling, op. cit.
37. Ibid.
38. Gordon Lindsay, *The Life of John Alexander Dowie* (Dallas: The Voice of Healing Pub. Co., 1951).
39. D. E. Harrell Jr., op. cit.
40. H. Davies, *The Challenge of the Sects* (Philadelphia: The Westminster Press, 1964).
41. J. T. Nichol, *Pentecostalism* (New York: Harper & Row, 1966).
42. Ibid.
43. Klaude Kendrick, *The Promise Fulfilled* (Springfield, Mo.: Gospel Pub. House, 1961)
44. Ibid.
45. J. T. Nichol, op. cit.
46. Ibid., p. 31.

47. Lately Thomas, *Storming Heaven* (New York: William Morrow & Co., 1970)
48. "New Life for the 'Old-Time Religion'," *U. S. News & World Report*, Oct. 19, 1970.
49. "Test for Big Churches: The Rise of Evangelism, Mysticism," *U. S. News & World Report*, Dec. 17, 1973, p. 43.
50. James Robinson, " 'Charismatic' Movement Faces Growing Rift," *Chicago Tribune*, Oct. 11, 1975.
51. James Robinson, " 'New Religions' Fading: Historian," *Chicago Tribune*, Jan. 31, 1976.
52. K. Kendrick, op. cit.
53. D. E. Harrell Jr., op. cit.
54. Gordon Lindsay, *The Gordon Lindsay Story* (Dallas: The Voice of Healing Pub. Co., [n. d.]).
55. Ibid.
56. D. E. Harrell Jr., op. cit., p. 30.
57. D. E. Harrell Jr., op. cit.
58. Ibid.
59. Ibid.
60. Ibid.
61. Ibid.
62. Ibid.
63. Ibid.
64. Ibid.
65. Ibid.
66. A. Spragett, op. cit.
67. "Healing in the Spirit," *Christianity Today*, July 20, 1973.
68. Russell Chandler, "No 'Second Miss Kuhlman' Apparent," *Los Angeles Times*, March 1, 1976.
69. *Los Angeles Times*, Feb. 21, 1976.
70. Russell Chandler, "Kuhlman Recovering from Surgery," *Los Angeles Times*, Jan. 10, 1976.
71. Ibid.
72. *The South Bend Tribune*, Sept. 22, 1975.
73. *Christianity Today*, Aug. 8, 1975.
74. R. Chandler, "Kuhlman Recovering etc."
75. *Los Angeles Times*, Feb. 21, 1976.
76. R. Chandler, "Kuhlman Recovering etc."
77. *Los Angeles Times*, Feb. 21, 1976.

78. R. Chandler, "No 'Second Miss Kuhlman' etc."

79. Steven S. Gaines, *Marjoe* (New York: Dell Pub. Co., Inc., 1973), pp. 7–8.

80. Eve Simson, "Becoming a Deliverance Evangelist: Impact of Socio-Economic Background and Personality Traits on Career Choice"; paper presented at the annual convention of the Association for Sociology of Religion, San Francisco, 1975.

81. Thomas Sowell, *Race and Economics* (New York: David McKay Co., Inc., 1975).

82. Glenn Norbal, "Negro Religion and Negro Status in the United States," *Religion, Culture & Society*, ed. Louis Schneider (New York: John Wiley & Sons, 1964), pp. 623–639.

83. John B. Holt, "Holiness Religion, Cultural Shock and Social Reorganization," *American Sociological Review*, Oct. 5, 1940.

84. M. M. Baker, *Broncos, Bulls, and Broken Bones* (Dallas: W. V. Grant, [n.d.]), pp. 1–3.

85. *Little David's Life Story* ([n.p., n.d.]).

86. Gordon Lindsay, *William Branham: A Man Sent from God* (Dallas: The Voice of Healing Pub. Co., 1950), pp. 32–33.

87. Velmer J. Gardner, *My Life Story* (Springfield, Mo.: Velmer J. Gardner, 1954), p. 4.

88. John Shelton Reed, *The Enduring South: Subcultural Persistence in Mass Society* (Lexington, Mass,: D. C. Heath and Co., 1972).

89. Charles H. Anderson, *White Protestant Americans: From National Origins to Religious Group* (Englewood Cliffs, N. J.: Prentice-Hall, 1970).

90. Charles Young, *Why I Preach in Sack Cloth* (Dallas: W. V. Grant, ([n.d.]), p. 2.

91. A. A. Allen, *Born to Lose, Bound to Win* (New York: Doubleday, 1970), p. 54.

92. Ralph Hart, *Doctors Pronounced Me Dead in Dallas* (Detroit: Ralph Hart, [n. d.]), p. 17.

93. Don Stewart and Walter Wagner, *The Man from Miracle Valley* (The Great Horizon Company, 1971), p. 35.

94. Ibid., p. 40.

95. Leroy Jenkins, *I Met the Master at the Crossroads*

(Tampa: Leroy Jenkins Evangelistic Association, Inc., 1965), p. 30.

96. P. W. Musgrave, "Towards a Sociological Theory of Occupational Choice," *Sociological Review*, 15, 1967.

97. G. M. Farley, *Sent by God* (Baltimore: Faith in Action, [n. d.]).

98. W. V. Grant, *The Gifts of the Spirit in the Home* (Dallas: W. V. Grant, [n. d.]), p. 11.

99. *The Voice of Deliverance*, March 1971, p. 8.

100. W. V. Grant, *The Grace of God in My Life* (Dallas: W. V. Grant, [n. d.]), pp. 16–17.

101. Bea Medlin, *Supernatural Ministry of Bea Medlin* (Dallas: W. V. Grant, [n. d.]), p. 2.

102. David Nunn, *The Life and Ministry of Evangelist David Nunn* (Dallas: David Nunn, [n. d.]), p. 2.

103. L. Jenkins, op. cit., p. 16.

104. M. M. Baker, op. cit., p. 9.

105. W. V. Grant, *The Grace of God in My Life*, p. 26.

106. A. Spragett, op. cit., p. 134.

107. Tommy Osborn Jr., *Back from Hell* (Dallas: W. V. Grant, [n. d.]), pp. 13–14.

108. G. Lindsay, *The Gordon Lindsay Story*.

109. Dallas Plemmons, *Captured by the Head Hunters* (Dallas: W. V. Grant, [n. d.]), p. 1.

110. W. V. Grant, *The Gifts of the Spirit in the Home*, p. 11.

111. *The Little Michael Story* (Dallas: W. V. Grant, [n. d.]).

112. Bud Chambers, *My Life Story Is a Song* (Oklahoma City, Okla.: Bud Chambers, [n. d.]).

113. C. A. Roberts, *Vic Coburn: Man with the Healing Touch* (Nashville & New York: Thomas Nelson, Inc., 1975).

114. D. Stewart and W. Wagner, op. cit., p. 139.

115. D. E. Harrell Jr., op. cit.

116. C. Young, op. cit., p. 19.

117. S. S. Gaines, op. cit., pp. 222–223.

118. G. Lindsay, *The Gordon Lindsay Story*.

119. S. S. Gaines, op. cit.

120. Ibid.

121. G. Lindsay, *The Gordon Lindsay Story*.

122. S. S. Gaines, op. cit.

123. Ibid.
124. Gene Luptak, "Money Ills Beset Faith-Cure Center," *The Arizona Republic*, April 9, 1973.
125. Ibid.
126. Ibid.
127. Don Stewart, "I Want You to Know the Truth," *Miracle*, Feb. 1973.
128. G. Luptak, "Money Ills etc."
129. Ibid.
130. *Miracle*, July 1976.
131. C. A. Roberts, op. cit.
132. *Columbus Citizen-Journal*, July 13, 1966.
133. *Deliverance Magazine*, Sept./Nov. 1966, pp. 6, 10.
134. Oral Roberts, *The Call* (New York: Doubleday, 1972).
135. D. E. Harrell Jr., op. cit.
136. *Faith Digest*, Sept. 1975.
137. S. S. Gaines, op. cit.
138. J. T. Nichol, op. cit.
139. C. A. Roberts, op. cit.
140. Stanley Howard Frodsham, *Smith Wigglesworth: Apostle of Faith* (Springfield Mo.: Gospel Pub. House, 1948).
141. James Dunn, *The Sign-Gift Ministry* (Dallas: W. V. Grant, [n. d.]).
142. Neal Frisby, *Creative Miracles* (Dallas: W. V. Grant, [n. d.]), pp. 17–18.
143. Hayes B. Jacobs, "Oral Roberts: High Priest of Faith Healers," *Harper's*, 224, Feb. 1962, p. 42.
144. G. Lindsay, *The Gordon Lindsay Story*.
145. L. Jenkins, op. cit.
146. King James Version.
147. Erika Bourguignon and Luanna Pettay, "Spirit Possession, Trance, and Cross-Cultural Research" (unpub. paper; The Ohio State University).
148. Morton T. Kelsey, *Tongue Speaking* (New York: Doubleday, 1964).
149. D. Stewart and W. Wagner, op. cit., pp. 221–222.
150. R. Chandler, "No 'Second Miss Kuhlman' etc."
151. Mrs. W. V. Grant, *The Story of My Life as a Preacher's Wife* (Dallas: W. V. Grant, [n. d.]), p. 13.
152. Faith Digest, Sept. 1975.

153. J. Morris, op. cit.
154. Mrs. W. V. Grant, op. cit., pp. 18–23.
155. Ibid., p. 22.
156. Vernon Scott, "Evangelism Is 'Refined Show Biz'," *The South Bend Tribune,* Feb. 2, 1976.
157. Malanie DeVault, "Outspoken Evangelist Dreams of Becoming Bigger than Graham," *Columbus Dispatch,* Oct. 4, 1975.
158. *The South Bend Tribune,* Sept. 22, 1975.
159. Mrs. W. V. Grant, op. cit., p. 28.
160. J. Morris, op. cit., p. 10.
161. *The Healing Messenger,* Jan. 1968, p. 6.
162. J. T. Nichol, op. cit., p. 92.
163. Kathryn Kuhlman, *I Believe in Miracles* (Englewood Cliffs, N. J.; Prentice-Hall, 1962).
164. G. Lindsay, *The Gordon Lindsay Story,* p. 64.
165. Ibid., p. 204.
166. A. A. Allen, *Does God Heal Through Medicine?* (Miracle Valley, Ariz.: A. A. Allen, [n. d.]).
167. J. Morris, op. cit.
168. C. A. Roberts, op. cit.
169. R. Hart, op. cit., p. 49.
170. Ibid., p. 50.
171. D. Stewart and W. Wagner, op, cit., p. 198.
172. Gordon Lindsay, *Fire over the Holy Land* (San Diego, Calif.: World Evangelism, Inc., [n. d.]), p. 4.
173. L. Jenkins, op. cit., pp. 88–90.
174. Basil Miller, *Grappling with Destiny* (Los Angeles: Wings of Healing, Inc., 1962).
175. *God's Tabernacle Revival Crusade* ([n. p., n. d.]), p. 1.
176. *Abundant Life,* Aug. 1968.
177. *The Voice of Deliverance,* Aug. 1968.
178. *Evangelistic Times,* July—Sept. 1968, p. 5.
179. *The Voice of Deliverance,* Oct. 1967, p. 15.
180. *The Voice of Deliverance,* Dec. 1967, p. 4.
181. Ibid., p. 7.
182. *Harvest Call,* Dec. 1970.
183. *Abundant Life,* Sept. 1968.
184. S. S. Gaines, op. cit.
185. Anton T. Boisen, "Religion and Hard Times: A Study of Holy Rollers," *Social Action,* 5, March 15, 1939.

186. Howard Elinson, "The Implications of Pentecostal Religion for Intellectualism, Politics and Race Relations," *The American Journal of Sociology*, 70, Jan. 1965.

187. S. S. Gaines, op. cit.

188. William W. Wood, *Culture and Personality Aspects of the Pentecostal Holiness Religion* (The Hague: Mouton & Co., 1965).

189. H. Elinson, "The Implications of Pentecostal Religion etc."

190. C. H. Anderson, op. cit.

191. N. J. Demerath III, *Social Class in American Protestantism* (Chicago: Rand McNally & Co., 1965).

192. Robert N. Butler and Myrna I. Lewis, *Aging and Mental Health* (St. Louis: The C. V. Mosby Co., 1973), p. 92.

193. O. Roberts, *My Twenty Years of a Miracle Ministry*.

194. David O. Moberg, "Religion in Later Years," *The Daily Needs and Interests of Older People*, ed. Adeline M. Hoffman (Springfield, Ill.: Charles C. Thomas, 1970), pp. 175–191.

195. Ibid.

196. Herman J. Loether, *Problems of Aging*, 2d ed. (Belmont, Calif.: Dickensen Pub. Co., 1975).

197. Ewald W. Busse and Eric Pfeiffer, "Functional Psychiatric Disorders in Old Age," *Behavior and Adaptation in Late Life*, ed. E. W. Busse and E. Pfeiffer (Boston: Little, Brown & Co., 1969).

198. Ronald Kotulak, "Medic Tells Latest Health Peril: Retirement," *Chicago Tribune*, May 3, 1971.

199. Fred Cottrell, *Aging and the Aged* (Dubuque, Iowa: Wm. C. Brown Co., 1974).

200. H. J. Loether, op. cit.

201. "Religious Cults: Newest Magnet for Youth," *U. S. News & World Report*, June 14, 1976.

202. D. E. Harrell Jr., op. cit.

203. J. Morris, op. cit.

204. E. Franklin Frazier, *The Negro Church in America* (New York: Schocken Books, 1963).

205. S. S. Gaines, op. cit.

206. J. Morris, op. cit.

207. H. Elinson, "The Implications of Pentecostal Religion etc."

208. J. B. Holt, "Holiness Religion etc."

209. Keith H. Basso, *The Cibecue Apaches* (New York: Holt, Rinehart & Winston, 1970).

210. Ibid.

211. S. S. Gaines, op. cit.

212. Robert Allerton Parker, *The Incredible Messiah* (Boston: Little, Brown & Co., 1937), pp. 136–138.

213. Carey McWilliams, *Southern California Country* (New York: Duell, Sloan & Pearce, 1946).

214. Ibid., p. 258.

215. John P. Kildahl, *The Psychology of Speaking in Tongues* (New York: Harper & Row, 1972).

216. Berthold E. Schwarz, "Ordeal by Serpents, Fire and Strychnine," *Psychiatric Quarterly*, 34, 1960.

217. "The Charismatic Movement and the Lutheran Church," a report of the Commission on Theology and Church Relations, The Lutheran Church— Missouri Synod, Jan. 1972.

218. J. P. Kildahl, op. cit.

219. B. E. Schwarz, "Ordeal by Serpents, Fire and Strychnine."

220. S. S. Gaines, op. cit., p. 202.

221. Carroll Stegall and Carl C. Harwood, *The Modern Tongues and Healing Movement* (The Western Bible Institute, [n. d.]).

222. David N. Mitchell, "City Has Been Hospitable to Valdez," *Milwaukee Journal*, March 27, 1968.

223. S. S. Gaines, op. cit.

224. J. Morris, op. cit., p. 29.

225. "Youth Action," *Miracle*, July 1971.

226. *Now*, May 1970.

227. Arnold M. Rose, "Reactions Against the Mass Society," *The Sociological Quarterly*, III, 4, Oct. 1962.

228. Willis M. Brown, *The Life and Conversion of a Kentucky Infidel* (Anderson, Ind.: Gospel Trumpet Co., 1904), p. 166.

229. G. Lindsay, *William Branham: A Man Sent from God*, p. 149.

230. C. Stegall and C. C. Harwood, *The Modern Tongues and Healing Movement*, pp. 16–18.

231. C. Stegall and C. C. Harwood, *The Modern Tongues and Healing Movement.*
232. "Coe's Cures," *Newsweek,* 47, Feb. 27, 1957.
233. "A Failure of Faith in a Faith Healer," *Life,* 40, March 5, 1956.
234. "Coe's Cures," *Newsweek,* 47, Feb. 27, 1957.
235. "A Failure of Faith in a Faith Healer," *Life,* 40, March 5, 1956.
236. D. E. Harrell Jr., op. cit.
237. G. Lindsay, *The Life of John Alexander Dowie.*
238. O. K. Armstrong, "Beware the Commercialized Faith Healer," *Reader's Digest,* June 1971, p. 186.
239. D. Richard Wolfe, "Faith Healing and Healing Faith," *Journal of the Indiana Medical Association,* 53, April 1959.
240. William A. Nolen, *Healing: A Doctor in Search of a Miracle* (New York: Random House, 1974), pp. 286–287.
241. Louis Rose, *Faith Healing* (Penguin Books, 1970).
242. Roy Hieger, "Divine Healing," *The Journal of the Kansas Medical Society,* 58, Dec. 1957.
243. C. C. Cawley, *The Right to Live* (New York: A. S. Barnes and Co., 1969).
244. O. K. Armstrong, "Beware the Commercialized Faith Healer."
245. Leslie D. Weatherhead, *Psychology, Religion and Healing* (Nashville: Abingdon-Cokesbury Press, [n. d.]), p. 197.
246. Arno Clemens Gaebelein, *The Healing Question* (New York: Our Hope Publication Office, 1925), p. 93.
247. C. C. Cawley, op. cit.
248. Ibid.
249. O. Roberts, *The Call.*
250. C. C. Cawley, op. cit.
251. Ibid.
252. O. K. Armstrong, "Beware the Commercialized Faith Healer," *Reader's Digest,* June 1971, p. 182.
253. V. Scott, "Evangelism Is 'Refined Show Biz'."
254. C. Stegall and C. C. Harwood, *The Modern Tongues and Healing Movement.*

255. O. K. Armstrong, "Beware the Commercialized Faith Healer," *Reader's Digest,* June 1971, p. 184.
256. C. Stegall and C. C. Harwood, *The Modern Tongues and Healing Movement.*
257. D. E. Harrell Jr., op. cit.
258. C. Stegall and C. C. Harwood, *The Modern Tongues and Healing Movement.*
259. L. Rose, op. cit.
260. W. A. Nolen, *Healing: A Doctor in Search of a Miracle,* p. 73.
261. W. A. Nolen, *Healing: A Doctor in Search of a Miracle.*
262. C. C. Cawley, *The Right to Live,* op. cit.
263. Robert Rawitch, "Evangelist Convicted in Auto Theft Case," *Los Angeles Times,* Jan. 20, 1976.
264. Robert Rawitch, "Evangelist Gets Probation, Fine in Car Theft Case," *Los Angeles Times,* March 3, 1976.
265. O. K. Armstrong, "Beware the Commercialized Faith Healer," *Reader's Digest,* June 1971, p. 183.
266. J. Morris, op. cit.
267. D. E. Harrell Jr., op. cit.
268. C. C. Cawley, op. cit.
269. "The Charismatic Movement and the Lutheran Church," a report of the Commission on Theology and Church Relations, The Lutheran Church—Missouri Synod, Jan. 1972, p. 26.
270. "Religious Quackery," *Time,* 79, Feb. 9, 1962.
271. Beverly Stumpf, "Faith Healing," unpub. paper, The Ohio State University, 1966, pp. 2–3.
272. John Pitts, *Faith Healing: Fact or Fiction* (Old Tappan, N. J.: Fleming H. Revell Co., [n. d.]).
273. B. Stumpf, "Faith Healing."
274. "Religious Quackery," *Time,* 79, Feb. 9, 1962.
275. W. A. Nolen, *Healing: A Doctor in Search of a Miracle.*
276. J. Pitts, op. cit.
277. Arthur J. Snider, "How Religion Helps to Heal," *Science Digest,* 59, July 1964,
278. Carl Brumback, *Suddenly from Heaven* (Springfield, Mo.: The Gospel Publishing Co., 1961), p. 334.
279. C. Brumback, *Suddenly from Heaven.*
280. D. Stewart and W. Wagner, op. cit., p. 149.

281. G. Lindsay, *William Branham: A Man Sent from God*.
282. D. E. Harrell Jr., op. cit.
283. Ibid.
284. G. Lindsay, *William Branham: A Man Sent from God*, pp. 194–195.
285. D. E. Harrell Jr., op. cit., p. 100.
286. Phil Dessauer, "God Heals—I Don't," *Coronet*, 38, Oct. 1955.
287. Jack Coe, *The Story of Jack Coe* (Dallas: Herald of Healing, Inc., 1955), p. 111.
288. C. A. Roberts, op. cit.
289. William A. Nolen, "In Search of a Miracle," *McCall's*, Sept. 1974, p. 104.
290. "Miracle Woman," *Time*, Sept. 14, 1970, p. 62.
291. A. Spragett, op. cit.
292. H. Richard Casdorph, *The Miracles* (Plainfield, N. J.: Logos International, 1976).
293. Ibid., p. 164.
294. Ibid., pp. 55–56, 165.
295. L. Salzman, "Spiritual and Faith Healing," *Journal of Pastoral Care*, 11, 1957.
296. L. Rose, op. cit.
297. Ibid.
298. D. E. Harrell Jr., op. cit.
299. Ibid.
300. C. A. Roberts, op. cit.
301. D. E. Harrell Jr., op. cit.
302. D. Stewart and W. Wagner, op. cit., pp. 222, 234.
303. D. E. Harrell Jr., op. cit.
304. Ibid., p. 236.
305. D. E. Harrell Jr., op. cit.
306. Ibid.
307. Ibid., p. 236.
308. D. E. Harrell Jr., op. cit.
309. Emily Gardiner Neal, *A Report Finds God Through Spiritual Healing* (New York: Morehouse-Gorham Co., 1956), pp. 111–112.

Index

age
  of believers in deliverance evangelism, 129-31
  of deliverance evangelists, 75

Allen, A.A., 42, 54, 64, 71, 78, 79, 87, 89-90, 97, 99, 111, 126, 133, 150, 155, 178

Allen, Lexie, 99

American Indians, 133-35

American Medical Association, 165

Angelus Temple, 25, 36

antagonists, as type of follower, 154-62
  consequences, 157-58
  methods used by, 154-57
  story of, 158-62

Armstrong, O.K., 173, 174

Assemblies of God, 43

Azusa Street Mission, 38

Baker, M.M., 50-51, 63

Barnes, G.O., 28-30, 178

"being saved," 91-93

belonging, sense of, as need of followers, 142

Ben Gurion, David, 24

Bethel Healing Home (Topeka), 33

Bible, 27, 179

birthplace, becoming deliverance evangelist and, 49-50

blacks, as believers in deliverance evangelism, 131-33

Boisen, Anton T., 126

Boone, Pat, 127

Bosworth, B.B., 32

Bosworth, F.F., 32, 38, 85, 156

Branham, William Marrion, 26, 27, 39-40, 51

Brant, Roxanne, 14, 45

British Medical Association, 167

Brown, Willis, 154, 178

Brumback, Carl, 182

Burchan, Lewin, 89

California, popularity of deliverance evangelism in, 135-37

Casdorph, Dr. H. Richard, 189-90

Chambers, Bud, 66, 120, 177-78

Chandler, Russell, 44

charlatans, deliverance evangelists as, 163-70

217